A Bainton Bibliography

BAINTON
BIBLIOGRAPHY

CYNTHIA WALES LUND

Copyright © 2000 Truman State University Press, Kirksville, MO 63501
www2.truman.edu/tsup
All rights reserved.
Printed in the United States of America

Habent sua fata libelli

Sixteenth Century Essays & Studies, Vol. XLVII

Raymond A. Mentzer, General Editor

Library of Congress Cataloging-in-Publication Data
Lund, Cynthia Wales, 1949–
     A Bainton bibliography / by Cynthia Wales Lund.
     p.   cm. – (Sixteenth century essays & studies : v. 47)
Includes index.
ISBN 0-943549-66-3 (alk. paper)
     1. Bainton, Roland Herbert, 1894– —Bibliography. I. Title. II.
Series.
Z8065.58.L86 1998
[BR139.B]   98-377
081—dc21   CIP

Cover Design: Teresa Wheeler, Truman State University Designer
Text: Adobe Garamond 10/13
∞The paper in this publication meets or exceeds the minimum requirements of the American
National Standard for Permanence of Paper for Printed Library Materials Z39.48 (1984).

To the memory of Roland Herbert Bainton
1894–1984

CONTENTS

WORKS ABOUT ROLAND H. BAINTON

ACKNOWLEDGMENTS

I WAS PRIVILEGED to have worked in the company of Roland H. Bainton and with his assistance from 1974 until 1980 when the original bibliography was completed. Such acquaintance made my compiling this bibliography a unique experience.

Martha Lund Smalley, Research Services Librarian and Curator of the Day Missions Collection at the Yale Divinity School Library, provided invaluable help from the beginning of the project in 1974 until its publication. She made practical use of the original 1980 bibliography when organizing the Roland H. Bainton Papers together with Nathan H. Price. The Papers have subsequently contributed to the expansion of the bibliography to its present form. Thanks also go to her staff for Xeroxing and providing answers to research questions,

Appreciation is offered to several colleagues in the library world who supported this project in its early stages: Kenneth E. Rowe, John A. Bollier, Stephen L. Peterson, and Forrest E. Brown. The initial encouragement to expand and publish the original bibliography came from John A. Tedeschi. I am grateful to Robert V. Schnucker, director emeritus of Truman State University Press, for agreeing to publish the bibliography. I also wish to thank his graduate student, Bryan Randal Reeves, for offering information and sharing his master's thesis about Roland Bainton. Paula Presley of Truman State University Press gave editorial advice and support while guiding the manuscript to its final form. I am grateful to Herbert Bainton, son of Roland H. Bainton, for permission to use his father's drawings.

Personal thanks go to my parents, Lincoln and Gretchen Wales, and parents-in-law, Kathryn and Gunnar Lund, for their ongoing support of my work over many years. My children, Karsten and Hannah, have given me computer assistance needed to produce this text. I have also appreciated the help and advice given by Janet Collrin and her student assistants in the Academic Computer Center at St. Olaf College.

Anne C. Tedeschi and Begonya Saez Tajafuerce have provided encouragement and inspiration by their ongoing commitment to careful scholarship.

Finally, I would like to offer special gratitude to my husband, Eric Lund, professor of religion at St. Olaf College, who as a church historian has shared my interest in the life and work of Roland Bainton. He has accompanied me during the twenty-six years of this project with patience and understanding.

Portrait of Roland H. Bainton painted by Deane Keller, professor emeritus of drawing and painting at Yale University. Unveiled 19 February 1975. Used by permission of Yale Divinity School.

INTRODUCTORY WORD
FOR THE BIBLIOGRAPHY

by Roland H. Bainton

I HEARD OF A MAN who desired as his epitaph, "He read the bibliographies." The first step in any work of scholarship is to find out what others have done. Of this I am so fully persuaded that I brought out a little booklet of works in English about the Reformation. It was so useful that my student and friend Eric Gritsch reissued it later trebled in size.

One who scans the present bibliography of my writings will gasp that I have been brash enough to dabble at so much. There are two explanations. The first is that my interests are broad, the second that for over forty years I have taught the history of Christianity and there is not an element in western culture that in one way or another has not been affected by Christian ideas. My biography of the heretic Michael Servetus led me into the history of medicine because apart from his heresy he was the discoverer of the pulmonary circulation of the blood. A book on Christian attitudes toward war and peace involved me in international law. A work on the treatment of Christ in art has taken me into the whole field of art history. And when it comes to what Christianity says about sex, love, and marriage, where won't that take one?

Because I revel in drawing and painting I have in a way illustrated some of my books. In a scholarly work I do not of course tamper with illustrations, but in a history of the Church for children I extracted from complicated pictures just which was to be explained. Here, for example, [see following page]. A tug of war between an angel and a devil [fig. 1] is extracted from a Judgment Day scene crowded with people. In the case of Botticelli's Dante viewing hell, the face and hands of Dante [fig. 2] are quite enough without hell. And Luther in the pulpit preaching has in the original [fig. 3] to our left the crucifix, the Lamb of God with a banner, the administration of the Lord's Supper with both the bread and the wine given to the lay folk. On the other side of Luther we have pope, cardinals, bishops, and monks going down hell's mouth. The bottom of the pulpit is partly covered by the heads of the parishioners. I snipped off their heads and drew their side of the pulpit to match the other

Fig. 1. Angel and devil in a tug of war on Judgment Day, by Roland H. Bainton. Used by permission of Herbert Bainton.

Fig. 2. Head and hands of Dante viewing hell (after Botticelli), by Roland H. Bainton. Used by permission of Herbert Bainton.

[fig. 4]. In the case of children what's the use of showing more than one is of a mind to explain?

I regret that my incompetence has not enabled me to deal with the church and music save to translate some hymns, which others have set to music. Social questions have always engaged me: in addition to war and peace, sex and marriage. I have dealt with religious liberty, alcoholism, the place of women in society and in the Church. So many fascinating subjects remain untouched that I could well use another eighty-five years to catch up. But one does have to leave something for one's successors to do and I am profoundly grateful for all the fascinating fields that I have been privileged to fringe.

Spring 1979
New Haven, Connecticut

Fig. 3. Sixteenth-century woodcut of Luther preaching.

Fig. 4. Bainton's rendition of Luther preaching. Used by permission of Herbert Bainton.

[xiii]

INTRODUCTION

THIS BIBLIOGRAPHY is a reflection of the life and work of one man, a major figure in the field of Reformation studies. Because Roland H. Bainton is significant in the study of sixteenth-century European history, this compilation is appropriately placed in the Sixteenth Century Essays and Studies Series. However, my effort to provide a bibliographic record is different in substance from many of the titles in this series which offers such an interesting array of historical research and original interpretation by distinguished scholars. Therefore, my work is presented with considerable humility, finally completed for publication so long after it was started. In the meantime, Roland Bainton has died, but, as the bibliography will illustrate, his influence on the scholarly world and upon us as individuals continues more than fifteen years after his death in 1984. It is with a sense of the living past continuing to shape our present that this bibliography is offered as a research tool for the future.

The original bibliography was compiled between 1974 and 1980. While serving as acquisitions librarian at the Yale Divinity School Library from 1974–79, I had access to most of the resources necessary for adding to the existing bibliography concerning Roland Bainton. My own interest in the subject developed earlier at Brown University where, as an undergraduate with a religious studies major, I was fortunate to have former students of Roland Bainton as my professors. I also enjoyed Bainton's book for young people, *The Church of Our Fathers*, as a girl growing up in a New England Congregational Church setting.

I was given a key to his office in Sterling Memorial Library at Yale when Roland Bainton accepted my offer to assist him with listing his works. It was a memorable experience to spend hours alone there going through his voluminous piles and boxes of articles and book reviews which were informally but well organized. The high ceiling in this Gothic-style building allowed space for hundreds of books, primarily titles on Renaissance and Reformation history. Lying between their pages were handwritten letters and notes from other great historians, often in German, French, or Italian. This room was full of treasures documenting the discussions and debates and personal associations of those who made it their mission in life to interpret the history of the Reformation period for twentieth-century people.

This bibliography thus took its shape from my direct contacts with Roland Bainton, from searching through his own materials, and from making use of the resources of the Yale libraries which had provided him with such wonderful support for his research. With his help, attempts were made to publish the original bibliography in 1980 but without success. The possibility of including it in the eventual publication of his autobiography also did not materialize. The early bibliography was put to use and corrected when the Bainton papers were organized by Martha Lund Smalley at the Yale Divinity School Library in 1992. The creation of this carefully organized archive insured that valuable resources from Roland Bainton's Sterling Library office were safely protected along with his other papers. The Roland H. Bainton Papers have been important in completing the final stages of this project.

My later work has all been done at St. Olaf College where I am currently Assistant Curator of the Howard V. and Edna H. Hong Kierkegaard Library. To find titles published since 1980, I have consulted various resources; especially the OCLC cataloging database and indexes, the *ATLA Religion Database on CD-ROM, Historical Abstracts on Disc,* various national books-in-print sources, and Internet searches. I have also consulted critical works published about Roland Bainton since his death and other bibliographies. Because Bainton's works have been translated into at least 15 languages and because he was reported in the popular press on many occasions and in many places, no bibliography of Bainton can be totally complete. However, I hope this compilation includes most materials relating to Roland H. Bainton.

I am not going to provide a biography of Roland Bainton in this introduction. A listing of events in his life is included as a guide. However, after considering the bibliography in its entirety, one can make some conclusions about the contributions of Roland Bainton and who he was as a person.

First of all, one can see that he was working as a scholar on an international level. Two of his books were originally published in Europe. Most of his works have been translated into numerous other languages. He was himself a translator. His articles appeared in foreign journals and books as well as in British and American publications. His introductions and forewords reflect his associations with an international community of scholars.

In their very interesting book, *The Reformation in Historical Thought*, A. G. Dickens and John M. Tonkin, with Kenneth Powell, have placed Bainton in a long line of historians of the Reformation period going back to the Reformation itself.[1] Bainton joined his predecessors in the sixteenth century who were writing as contemporaries of the Reformation in Europe as well as his own colleagues in the twentieth century. Both groups formed associations crossing the boundaries of language

---

1. A. G. Dickens and John Tonkin with Kenneth Powell, *The Reformation in Historical Thought* (Cambridge: Harvard Press, 1985).

and nation. Miriam Usher Chrisman in her "In Memoriam" has noted the importance of Bainton's relationships with German, Swiss, and French scholars which resulted in the revival of the *Archiv für Reformationsgeschichte*, a journal published with the joint cooperation of the Verein für Reformationsgeschichte in Europe and the American Society for Church History.[2] As this bibliography shows, the number of articles and reviews which Roland Bainton contributed to this journal alone bears witness to his commitment to international scholarship and his participation on advanced levels.

His international interests are also evident in the articles by and about him listed in the bibliography which relate less to his scholarship than to his own religious commitments and personal life. He expanded his interests from writing about the history of Europe for North American students and scholars to presenting his research to varied audiences in Latin America, Africa, and Asia. In his later years, he was still enjoying learning new languages. (He was able to read almost every European language as well as Hebrew, Greek, and Latin.) At the end of his life, his Christmas card list included over 700 people all over the world with whom he continued to keep in touch. His ability to interpret history using both the written and spoken word was extraordinary.

Roland Bainton's commitment to pacifism in World War I and his life-long work on behalf of world peace are another aspect of his international perspective reflected in the bibliography. He has been described as an historian of the peace movement by Steven H. Simpler in *Roland H. Bainton: An Examination of his Reformation Historiography*.[3] In 1979, Roland Bainton received the Gandhi Peace Award from the Promoting Enduring Peace organization. The inscription read, "With appreciation for your life-long commitment to peacemaking and opposing war. Through your teaching and speaking, your extensive travels, your many books on religion, history, and peace, and your service to numerous groups including Promoting Enduring Peace and the Religious Society of Friends, you have touched us all and made lasting contributions toward building world community."[4]

This bibliography also shows very clearly that Bainton worked for his entire life with the particular identity of a Christian scholar. As Simpler has explained, Bainton insisted on the importance of taking the religious aspect of human experience seriously when doing historical research.[5] His very conscious attempts to write historical works directed at the common person, the practicing Christian, are confirmed in the bibliography. For example, he enjoyed bringing Luther to modern Christians in the

2. OB1.
3. NB1, p. 195.
4. O20.3.
5. NB1, pp. 185–94.

form of a book for Christmas and another for Easter. As the articles in the bibliography show, Bainton wrote regularly for popular journals offering advice to Christian readers on issues of personal life in the modern world.

Also evident in the bibliography are Roland Bainton's primary commitments to the Congregational church, in which he was ordained, and to the Society of Friends (Quakers), with which he was formally associated. At the same time, the bibliography shows Bainton's commitment to ecumenism and religious toleration. His major work on Erasmus, who remained within the Roman Catholic church, is an example of his scholarship reflecting personal commitment. The Vatican Librarian is reported to have said, "What that man knows and has written about Luther is of inestimable value to the Catholic Church."[6] The bibliography lists books and articles which Bainton wrote concerning the medieval church and the early church confirming his interest in the larger church. He was able to maintain his sectarian commitments without losing sight of the historical context in which they had developed.

While working on an international level and with an ecumenical spirit, Roland Bainton was also an American scholar. The bibliography contains many entries documenting his role as spokesman and teacher on the current American scene. Perhaps most important was his nearly 70 years of association with Yale Divinity School, one of the nation's oldest institutions. Articles about him over many years abound in the publications of Yale University. This bibliography includes titles by Bainton which are historical studies of people and events in New Haven. His active involvement in current social issues throughout his life is also documented. His outspoken views during the McCarthy era and the Vietnam War attest to his intimate awareness of issues pressing on the collective conscience of Americans. His innumerable contributions to and contacts with students across the country, as well as at Yale, are also illustrated by citations in the bibliography.

Scholarly discussion within the United States on topics of Reformation history is documented. Bainton has been referred to by Dickens, Tonkin, and Powell as the "doyen of American historians of the Reformation who has illuminated so many sides of the subject that our belated tribute can scarcely do justice to one whose sheer humanity has attracted a huge readership in this field."[7] Many Americans have been touched by the work of Roland Bainton. His interest in biography as an historical genre and his style of writing made possible the popularization of Reformation history in North America. In his thesis entitled *Roland H. Bainton: The Historian as Social Activist*, Brian Randal Reeves has quoted Bainton as saying, "The scholar, the writer, the poet, the preacher are all obliged to reach the people."[8] Perhaps Roland

6. OB4, p. 6 (Raymond Morris).
7. NB3
8. S2.

Bainton saw it as his duty to "reach the people" but it was also his rare gift to be able to do so.

One of Roland H. Bainton's most original and significant contributions historically was his breaking new ground in areas which had been previously undocumented in Reformation studies. Bainton coined the phrase "the left wing of the Reformation"[9] to describe those reformers outside the traditional areas of study surrounding Luther and Calvin. He was the first to offer major studies of Ochino, Servetus, Castellio, and Joris. He was also the first to present studies of women of the Reformation. Bainton's interest in the figures of the left wing of the Reformation reflect clearly his passionate interest in the expression of individual conscience particularly with regard to religious conviction.

Both his scholarly and more popular writings represented in the bibliography illustrate his interest in liberty of conscience and religious freedom.[10] In an article in *Gospel Herald*, Gregory I. Jackson has written, "The labors of Bainton have given America scores of energetic and tolerant historians, many of whom have continued his research on the Anabaptists and the radicals…. Because of Roland Bainton, millions have come to appreciate the contributions of the sixteenth-century prophets. He [Bainton] comments, 'All I can say is that I may have done a lot of sparking. But more important is the change in interest in our time which sees its antecedents in the rebels of the past.'"[11]

Simpler has also noted the tie between Bainton's personal interest in the common man and his choice of historical subjects. "Bainton's interest is in the unheralded prophet, in the exploited religious groups, and with the hearty souls hidden in historical anonymity. It appears as a historiographical concern to do justice to such people in his own writings."[12] Bainton's articles on concerns of the pastoral ministry, popular faith and preaching, teaching, and on matters of the family confirm this observation and are listed in the bibliography.

I hope that aside from information about Bainton's career and historical corpus, anyone reading this bibliography and consulting its titles will also discover the unique individual who was their author. The bibliography's books and articles about Bainton reveal his particularly appealing and special character: "The archetype of all real bicycling professors"[13]; "A professor whose teaching style was "discipline plus encouragement"[14]; A distinguished theologian with "his rare combination of pas-

---

9. NB1, p. 224. A discussion on terminology concerning the "left wing" is also found in Simpler's study, NB1, pp. 113–19.

10. Bainton discusses these aspects in his autobiography; A39, p. 77.

11. O16.3, p. 802.

12. S3, p. 174.

13. O29; see "The Bicycling Professor," p. 3.

14. O21; see "Man of Many Faces," by John Knoble, p. 23..

sion for perfection with outgoing friendliness, warmth of personality by which he touched the lives and quickened the minds of an innumerable host of persons"[15]; "His essential humanity and friendliness to students"[16]; "The warm, creative, unassuming nature of this Luther scholar.... Artist, lecturer, mimic, punster, lover of children, family man, poet, visionary, cook, pastor, and social activist...unpretentious and warm host."[17]; "In the complicated babble of history, Roland Bainton has remained one of God's humble and profound children."[18] Bainton himself liked being described by his former student, Fred Meek of Old South Church, Boston, as "part Puck, part Saint Francis, with a mixture of Erasmus, gathered up in a mold provided for him by his English clergyman father."[19]

In his autobiography, Bainton describes his journey by ship and train in the 1920's to use European libraries. To facilitate his research, he carried a heavy typewriter in his backpack.[20] This image of Roland Bainton as a young man has accompanied me while completing the final stages of my work on this bibliography. Now we can "enter" these same libraries via the Internet, locating at least the titles of their holdings from our own homes. In some cases, we can read texts at long distance. I have wondered how Roland Bainton would have responded to the "age of information." This bibliography documents his adoption of a variety of mediums to convey his historical message. Most likely he would have adapted to and made use of what we now have as tools for research with his characteristic enthusiasm and energy.

Bainton is himself a subject for search, a "hit" on the World Wide Web, at various locations. During one search under the term "Roland H. Bainton," I was directed to the on-line course bulletin of an Italian university. In this catalog was listed a course on Erasmus. Bainton's book on Erasmus, in an Italian translation, was listed as a required text. Likewise, the Web alerted me to the Roland H. Bainton Book Prizes, fitting memorials sponsored by the Sixteenth Century Studies Conference. The University of Virginia was announcing a ceremony at which this annual honor was awarded.[21]

Methods of historical research have changed since Roland Bainton put out his own "little booklet of works in English about the Reformation."[22] However, the paths to understanding of the history of the Reformation in the twenty-first century

15. O21.
16. O29; see "Bicyclist Bainton," p. 4.
17. O12, p. 3.
18. O12, p. 4.
19. O32.8 and O21; see "Rev. R. H. Bainton, Bike-riding Author, Caricaturist, Retiring After 43 Years."
20. A39, p. 82.
21. OM1.
22. "Introductory Word for the Bibliography," p. xi.

will of necessity retrace the routes mapped out in the twentieth century by Roland Bainton and other "pioneers." I hope this bibliography will serve as a useful bridge to understanding for all those trying to interpret the complexity and controversy of sixteenth-century Reformation history which Roland H. Bainton revealed to so many in the twentieth century. I also hope that it will provide insight into how one man interpreted the way to religious toleration and world peace in our time simply by living a life in keeping with his beliefs and generously sharing his personal gifts.

January 2000
St. Olaf College
Northfield, Minnesota

Roland H. Bainton in his office, Sterling Memorial Library, Yale University. Photo used by permission, Yale Divinity School.

EVENTS IN THE LIFE OF ROLAND H. BAINTON

1894..... March 30. Born the only son of James Herbert Bainton, Congregational pastor, and Charlotte Blackham Bainton in Ilkeston, Derbyshire, England.

1898..... Moved to Vancouver, British Columbia.

1902..... Moved to Colfax, Washington.

1906..... Began the study of Latin.

1907..... Began the study of German.

1910..... Graduated from Colfax High School. Whitman College, Walla Walla, Washington.

1914..... Graduated from Whitman College. BA degree in Classics. Entered Yale Divinity School.

1917..... Graduated from Yale Divinity School. BD degree.

1918–19.. Declared pacifism serving without military rank in a unit of the American Friends Service Committee under the American Red Cross in France.

1920..... January. Appointed instructor in Church History and New Testament at Yale Divinity School.

1921..... Received Ph.D. degree in Semitics and Hellenistic Greek from Yale University. June 8: Married Ruth Mae Woodruff, a teacher.

1923..... Promoted to Assistant Professor. Dissertation published, *Basilidian Chronology and New Testament Interpretation.*

1926..... Awarded Guggenheim Fellowship. Studied in Swiss archives researching proponents of religious liberty during the Reformation.

1926–35.. Served as Librarian, Trowbridge Reference Library, Yale Divinity School.

1927..... Ordained as Congregational minister.

1930..... *Debtors to God* published.

1932..... Promoted to Associate Professor.

1935..... *Concerning Heretics* and *Bibliography of the Continental Reformation* published.

1935–62.. Appointed Titus Street Professor of Ecclesiastical History, Yale Divinity School, the third person to hold this chair following George P. Fischer and Williston Walker.

1936–39.. Facilitated the emigration of European scholars to the United States.

1937..... *David Joris* published.

1940..... Served as President of the American Society of Church History.

1941..... *Bernardino Ochino* and *Church of Our Fathers* published.

1943..... *George Lincoln Burr* published.

1944–45.. *The Panorama of the Christian Church* published.

1948..... Traveled to post-war Germany for the American Friends Service Committee.
Awarded honorary Doctor of Theology degree by the University of Marburg, the oldest Protestant Seminary in Germany.
Publication of *The Martin Luther Christmas Book*.

1949..... Awarded honorary Doctor of Divinity degree by Meadville Seminary.

1950..... *Here I Stand* published.
Received Abingdon-Cokesbury Award for *Here I Stand*.

1951..... *The Travail of Religious Liberty* published.

1951–69.. Cofounded *Archiv für Reformationsgeschichte* and served on its editorial board.

1952..... *The Reformation of the Sixteenth Century* published.

1953..... *Hunted Heretic* published. Awarded honorary Doctor of Divinity Degree by Oberlin College.

1954..... Awarded honorary Doctor of Divinity Degree by Whitman College.
Member of newly formed Renaissance Society, a continuing association.
The Covenant in the Wilderness published.
Friends in Relation to the Churches published.

1955–63.. Served on the Editorial Board of *Church History*.

1956..... *The Age of the Reformation* published.

1957..... *Yale and the Ministry* published.

1958..... Awarded honorary Doctor of Letters degree by Gettysburg College.
Awarded honorary Doctor of Humane Letters by Wilmington College.
Pilgrim Parson published.

1960..... *Christian Attitudes toward War and Peace* published.
Early Christianity published.
Became a member of the Heidelberger Akademie der Wissenschaften.
Traveled to South America.

1962   Retired from Yale Divinity School and Yale Graduate School faculty. Became Professor Emeritus.

       The Medieval Church published.

       Collected Papers in Church History: Series One published.

       Luther's Meditations on the Gospels published.

1963..... *Collected Papers in Church History: Series Two* published.

1964..... *Collected Papers in Church History: Series Three* published.

       The Horizon History of Christianity published.

1965..... Became a member of the Sociéte d'Histoire et d'Archéologie de Genève.

1966..... Traveled to Africa.

       Death of Ruth Woodruff Bainton.

1967..... Awarded honorary Doctor of Humane Letters by Wagner College.

       Traveled to Japan.

1968..... Became a member of the Société de l'Histoire du Protestantisme Française.

1969..... *Erasmus of Christendom* published.

       Traveled to England and Lebanon

1970..... Awarded the Wilbur Cross Medal by the Yale Graduate School.

       Awarded honorary Doctor of Letters degrees by Earlham College and Rocky Mountain College.

1971..... Traveled to Germany, Italy, Lebanon, Israel, Jordan, Turkey, and India.

       Women of the Reformation in Germany and Italy published.

1973..... Became a member of the British Academy.

       Women of the Reformation in France and England published.

1974..... Awarded an honorary Doctor of Humane Letters degree by New Haven University.

       Behold the Christ published.

1975..... Traveled to Poland as Chairman of the Yale Committee on Cultural Relations with Poland.

1976..... Traveled to Greece and Crete.

1977..... *Women of the Reformation from Spain to Scandinavia* published.

1978..... *Yesterday, Today, and What Next?* published.

       A Pilgrimage to Luther's Germany published.

1979..... Awarded Gandhi Peace Award by Promoting Enduring Peace organization.

1983..... *The Martin Luther Easter Book* published.

1984..... Death of Roland Herbert Bainton.

1988..... Autobiography, *Roly,* published by Yale Divinity School.

1990..... Roland H. Bainton Book Prize awarded for the first time by the Sixteenth Century Studies Conference. Given annually.

ACADEMIC MEMBERSHIPS
HELD BY ROLAND H. BAINTON

American Academy of Arts and Sciences
American Association of University Professors
American Historical Association
American Society of Church History
Foundation for Reformation Research
International Institute of Arts and Letters
Medieval Academy of America
Renaissance Society of America

Roland H. Bainton, "Self-Portrait," 1962

PUBLISHED MATERIALS
BY
ROLAND H. BAINTON

A. MONOGRAPHS

1923

A1   *Basilidian Chronology and New Testament Interpretation.* Leipzig: Drugulin, 1923. 53 pages.

Written as the author's Ph.D. dissertation for Yale University, this work was originally entitled "The Basilidian Gospel Chronology." It shows RHB's early interest in classical and biblical studies as well as the history of the Early Church. The work is extremely technical and includes frequent references in Greek. RHB examines the chronology and dating of Jesus' life as understood in the second century by Basilides and his sect. The historical and intellectual mileu forming Basilides' thought is clearly presented. RHB concludes that the Basilidian system was completely erroneous. The dissertation was viewed by its author as more significant for the field of New Testament interpretation than for the study of New Testament chronology.

— Reprinted from the *Journal of Biblical Literature,* 42:1–2 (1923): 81–134. See D1.

— Part extracted and included in *Collected Papers I,* pp. 29–38, under the title "The Origins of Epiphany." See A26.

1930

A2   *Debtors to God: Pioneers in the Christian Quest.* Philadelphia: Westminster, 1930. 80 pages (pupil's edition), 64 pages (teacher's edition). Westminster Departmental Graded Materials.

This work is one of a series in the Pioneer Program for Boys and Girls, ages twelve to fourteen, sponsored by the Presbyterian Church. Written in thirteen lessons to fit into a weekly church school program, RHB approaches the history of Protestantism with biographical sketches of thirteen individuals including John Hus, Martin Luther, several missionaries, and two women, one of whom is Harriet Beecher Stowe. Each lesson includes biographical narrative materials for a service of worship, and questions to think over and answer. The pupil's edition includes ten illustrations in the form of line drawings. The teacher's edition provides an introduction and short bibliography for each lesson but has only two illustrations.

1935

A3   *Bibliography of the Continental Reformation: Materials Available in English.* Chicago: American Society of Church History, 1935. 54 pages. Monographs in Church History, no. 1.

This contribution to the study of the Reformation was undertaken to answer "the needs of the student of the Reformation limited to English." Reviewers of the first edition termed this list "astonishingly complete" although RHB did not attempt to be all-inclusive. Topics not included in the early version are the English Reformation, precursors of the Reformation, and the Counter-Reformation. It was expected that advanced students would turn to established German bibliographies for further citations.

— Second edition, revised and enlarged. With Eric W. Gritsch. Hamden, Ct.: Archon Books, 1972. 220 pages.

— North Haven, Ct.: Shoe String Press, 1974. 220 pages.

The second edition follows closely the format of the first but was enlarged from 54 to 220 pages and refers to 116 instead of 58 journal titles. Gritsch indicates that he blended new references into the earlier edition making no pretense at completeness. Again, some topics were arbitrarily omitted in the later version, but new topics were added such as the Roman Catholic reform. A number of headings were changed responding to new scholarly interpretations of the reform movement. Sections were expanded and a table of contents added. Reviewers in 1974 anticipated a third edition, which apparently did not appear.

A4   *Concerning Heretics: Whether They Are to Be Persecuted and How They Are to Be Treated, A Collection of the Opinions of Learned Men, Both Ancient and Modern,* an anonymous work attributed to Sebastian Castellio, now first done into English together with excerpts from other works of Sebastian Castellio and David Joris on religious liberty, by Roland H. Bainton. New

York: Columbia University Press, 1935. 342 pages. Records of Civilization Sources and Studies, no. 22.

This scholarly work was the first to be published based on RHB's research findings gathered in 1926 during study funded by a Guggenheim fellowship. The year was spent largely in Swiss archives examining sources for a major study of four heretics who fled Catholic countries for Swiss cities only to be persecuted by Calvin's regime. The four figures examined were Joris of the Netherlands, Ochino of Italy, Castellio of France, and Servetus of Spain. A single-volume study of the four was never published. Instead, separate in-depth volumes have been presented. This volume deals with Sebastian Castellio.

Received by reviewers as a major contribution to the study of this figure, the work reflects great diligence and scholarly care. An introductory section deals with the occasion and authorship of Castellio's work including examination of the sources of Castellio's thought and the significance of his writing for the literature concerning religious liberty. The document itself is presented in fluent translation and is followed by excerpts from other works of Castellio and Joris. A full bibliography is included as well as an index. It is illustrated with portraits, woodcuts, paintings, and engravings from the period.

— Reprinted with a new introduction. New York: Octagon Books, 1965. 346 pages.

— New York: Hippocrene Books, 1965.

1937

A5   *David Joris: Wiedertäufer und Kämpfer für Toleranz im 16. Jahrhundert.* [Translated by Hajo Holborn and Annemarie Holborn.] Leipzig: M. Heinsius Nachfolger, 1937. 229 pages. *Archiv für Reformationsgeschichte.* Texte und Untersuchungen. Erganzungsband 6.

Written originally in English but published in German, this scholarly work is one of several based on research done by RHB in 1926 while studying on a Guggenheim fellowship. The author considered Joris the most provocative of the four heretics investigated although he was the least persecuted. The work became the authoritative biography and interpretation of Joris upon publication. It aimed to explain the reasons for Joris' ultimate involvement with the Anabaptists.

The first half of the book presents narrative on Joris as a pastor in the Netherlands and then at the Basel inquisition. The latter half presents many significant documents from the archives of Zurich and Basel relevant to the posthumous trial of Joris in the years 1558 to 1561. Bibliography relating to Joris' own writings and historical milieu are also included. A *Personenregister* serves as the only index. The work is not illustrated.

— Translated from unpublished English manuscript. Typescript. Roland H. Bainton Papers. Manuscripts and Archives, Yale Divinity Library. See Q2.

— Microform. "A Refugee from the Netherlands: David Joris." Zug: Inter Documentator, 19—. 118 pages on 2 microfiches. (The Radical Reformation Microfiche Project, section 1) "This is the original English version of the writing by Bainton which appeared in print in a German translation under the title: 'David Joris. Wiedertäufer und Kämpfer für Toleranz in 16 Jahrhundert' (1937).... From a comprehensive collection of the primary sources on religious conformity in Europe during the sixteenth century."

1941

A6   *Bernardino Ochino, Esule e Riformatore Senese del Cinquecento, 1487–1563*; Versione dal manoscritto inglese di Elio Gianturco. Firenze: Sansoni, 1941. 213 pages. Biblioteca Storica Sansoni, n.s. 4.

The third of RHB's studies on heretics stemming from research done in 1926, this volume was originally written in English but published in Italian as part of a new series directed by the well-known historian Federico Chabod. Other scholars who contributed to the series were Delio Cantimori, Johann Huizinga, and Armando Sapori.

This study was viewed at the time of its publication as the first major study of Ochino since Karl Benrath's important work, *Bernardino Ochino von Siena*, which appeared in 1875. RHB presents the external events surrounding Ochino's life and an evaluation of his religious thought. He also brings to light numerous new documents. Cited in the detailed bibliography are editions of Ochino's works, works by his contemporaries, and many more modern secondary works on Ochino and his times. The book is indexed and illustrated with glossy reproductions of sixteenth-century original woodcuts and engravings. A portrait of Ochino is included.

— Translated from unpublished English manuscript, "Bernardino Ochino of Siena." Typescript. 229 pages. Roland H. Bainton Papers. Manuscripts and Archives. Yale Divinity Library. See Q2.

— Microform of Italian translation. Waltham, Mass.: Graphic Micro-films of New England., Inc., 196–; 1 microfilm reel; positive: 16 mm. Starr King School of Ministry Rare Books.

A7   *The Church of Our Fathers.* New York: Scribner's, 1941. 248 pages.

Many Protestant young people in numerous countries have first met Roland Bainton through this work. Dedicated to his children and grandchildren, the book is a history of the church from the days of the Early Church until the arrival of Christians in North America. Combining RHB's scholarly approach to history with his ability to reach children through a combination of story and narrative, the work was received with enthusiasm upon publication. It is amply illustrated with line drawings by the author adapted from appropriate artistic sources from various periods. The inside covers provide chronological charts by century showing major figures and events. Although it was written for junior high school age students, the book makes interesting and delightful reading for adults as well as children.

— Reprinted, 1944.

— Reprinted, 1950. 221 pages.

— Special edition for Sunday schools. Philadelphia: Westminster, 1950. 219 pages.

— New revised edition. New York: Scribner's, 1953. 222 pages.

— Reprinted, 1955.

— New revised edition. New York: Scribner's, 1963. 221 pages.

— Paper edition. New York: Scribner's, 1969. 222 pages.

— Republished. New York: Scribner's, 1978. 222 pages.

— Paper edition. Englewood Cliffs, N.J.: Prentice-Hall, 1978. 222 pages.

— Republished. Magnolia: Peter Smith, 1984.

— Reprinted. Salem, Ohio: Schmul, 1987. 222 pages. Original Scribner 1941 edition.

— British edition. London: SCM, 1947. 248 pages.

— Chinese edition. [romanization] *Chi-tu chiao fa ta shih*. Translated by Cheng Po-ch'un i. Shanghai: Kuang hsūeh hui, 1948. 260 pages.

— French translation. *Notre église à deux mille ans*. Trad. André Péry. Genève: Labor et Fides; diffusion en France: Librairie Protestante, Paris, 1964. 224 pages.

— Hebrew translation. *Toldat ha-Natsrut*. Translated by Tsevi Rin. Tel Aviv: "Dugit," 1950. 218 pages.

— Korean translation. [romanization] *Chongt' ong kyohoesa*. Translated by Kim In-ch'ol yok. Seoul: Han'guk Kiddokkyo Kyoyuk Yon gu W on: 1981. 296 pages.

— Japanese translation. [romanization] *Sekai Kirisutoky-oshi*. Translated by Kega Shigemi. Tokyo: Kyo Bun Kwan, 1953. 299 pages.

— Republished. Tokyo: Kyo Bun Kwan, 1981.

— Spanish translation. *La Iglesia de nuestros padres*. Traducida par Laura Jorquera y A. F. Sosa. Buenos Aires: Editorial "La Aurora"; Mexico City: Casa Unida de Publicaciones, 1953. 249 pages.

— Third edition. Buenos Aires: La Aurora, 1975. c. 1969.

— Thai translation. Bangkok: Church of Christ in Thailand, 1955. 375 pages.

1943

A8   *George Lincoln Burr: His Life*, by Roland H. Bainton; Selections from His Writings edited by Lois Oliphant Gibbons. Ithaca: Cornell University Press, 1943. 505 pages.

This work honors a well-loved Cornell professor with whom RHB corresponded for ten years as a friend. His own thanks to Burr can be found in *Concerning Heretics* where he acknowledges Burr as his faithful correspondent. Lois Oliphant Gibbons, Burr's last Ph.D. student, selected materials that make up about two thirds of the volume. RHB wrote the first third, "Part 1: His Life," a 143–page biographical narrative. A bibliography of Burr's writings appears at the end of the volume compiled by Henry H. King of the Cornell University Library. A portrait of Burr serves as a frontispiece.

1944–1945

A9   *The Panorama of the Christian Church in Kodachrome Slides.* Selected and described by RHB. Photography by the Yale Divinity School Department of Visual Aids. Boston: Pilgrim Press, 1944. Accompanied by 150 Kodachrome slides in 2 boxes and 159–page guide. [Part 1. The Early and Eastern Churches (slides 1–31). Part 2. The Middle Ages (slides 32–93); Part 3. The Period of Reformation (slides 94–132). Part 4. The American and Younger Churches (slides 133–150). Paul Vieth, photographic director.]

This publication was written to describe the slides selected for this presentation of Christian history and serves as a leader's guide. RHB's gathering of material from Christian art illustrates his interest in art and his belief in its usefulness for historical study. The author personally made illustrations used in a number of the slides, which were photographed at the Yale Divinity School Department of Visual Arts. While this collection is directed to a general audience in a popular fashion, the explanatory materials reflect the scholarly research of the author.

1948

A10   *The Martin Luther Christmas Book*, with Celebrated Woodcuts by His Contemporaries. Translated and arranged by Roland H. Bainton. Philadelphia: Westminster and Philadelphia: Muhlenberg, 1948. 74 pages.

Those who heard RHB tell his annual Luther Christmas story at Yale Divinity School will not be surprised by this small and attractive book. He presents in narrative form excerpts from Luther's commentaries on the Christmas story showing clearly Luther's sensitivities to the experiences of Mary, Joseph, and the other participants. Luther's concern for making the Nativity real to people of his own time becomes clear. The book is illustrated with woodcuts by contemporaries of Luther.

— New edition. Philadelphia: Muhlenberg Press, 1959. 74 pages.

— Philadelphia: Fortress, 1968. 74 pages.

— Philadelphia, Fortress, 1984. 74 pages.

— Chinese translation.Translated by Joe Dunn. Hong Kong: Torosheng, 1965. 75 pages.

— Japanese translation. Tokyo: Shinkyo-Shuppansha, Protestant Publishing House, 1958 and 1964. 138 pages.

— [romanization] *Nakamura bukku.* Translated by Nakamura Taeko. Tokyo: Shinky-oshuppansha, 1983. 102 pages.

— Certain portions appear in condensed form in *Here I Stand.* See A11.

1950

A11   *Here I Stand: A Life of Martin Luther.* New York: Abingdon-Cokesbury, 1950. 422 pages.

RHB's most popular and widely read book was a major contribution to the field of Reformation studies, providing a definitive biography of Luther in English. It has been translated into numerous languages and reviewed in countless newspapers and periodicals. The 1982 seventh printing reportedly sold one million copies. The author received the Abingdon-Cokesbury Award in 1950 for this work.

Parts of this book were originally delivered as the Nathaniel Taylor Lectures at the Yale Divinity School (1946–47), The Carew Lectures at the Hartford Seminary Foundation (1949), and the Hein Lectures at Wartburg Seminary and Capital University. Parts were also presented at the Bonebrake Theological Seminary, Gettysburg Seminary, and the Divinity School of Howard University.

The work examines the life of Luther chronologically with elaboration throughout of the political, social, intellectual, and religious milieus governing Luther's thought and actions. The influence of Luther is addressed at the close of the book. It is heavily illustrated with black and white drawings of contemporary art works. An extensive bibliography lists secondary materials on Luther and his times. An index is provided.

— Paper edition. New York: Abingdon, 1950. 422 pages. Apex Books.

— New paper edition. New York: New American Library, 1955. 336 pages. Mentor Book, 127.

— New York: Abingdon, 1957.

— New York: New American Library, 1961.

— New York: Penguin Books USA, 1977. 336 pages. A Mentor Book.

— New York: New American Library, 1977 and 1978. 336 pages. A Mentor Book.

— Nashville: Abingdon, 1978. 336 pages. Festival Books.

— Nashville: Abingdon, 1990. 336 pages.

— Magnolia: Peter Smith, 1990.

— Nashville: Abingdon, 1991, paper edition.

— New York: Meridian, 1995 c. 1950. 336 pages.

— 1996 *Books in Print* lists 1955 edition available from NAL, Dutton.

— NAL, Dutton paper edition, *1996 Books in Print*. 288 pages.

— British edition. London: Hodder and Stoughton, 1951. 422 pages.

Tring, Hertfordshire: Lion, 1983 c. 1978. 412 pages. A Lion Paperback.

— Chinese translation. *Che shih wo ti li ch'ang: Kai chiao hsien tao Ma-ting Lu-te huan Chi = Here I Stand.* Translated by Lo lun P'ei-tengchu. Hong Kong: Taosheng, 1987. 480 pages.

Yilin Press, 1993. 369 pages.

— Finnish translation. *Täss ä Seison: Martti Lutherin el äm ä.* Helsinki: SLEY-Kirjag Oy, 1982. 362 pages.

— German translation. *Hier Stehe Ich: Das Leben Martin Luthers.* Berechtigte Übersetzung aus dem Amerikanischen von Hermann Dörries. Göttingen: Duerlichsche Verlagsbuchhandlung, 1952. 367 pages.

2. Auflage. *Martin Luther.* Berechtigte Übersetzung aus dem Amerikanischen von Hermann Dörries. Göttingen: Vandenhoeck & Ruprecht, 1958. 367 pages.

3. Auflage. *Martin Luther.* Göttingen: Vandenhoeck & Ruprecht, 1959. 367 pages.

6. neubearbeitete Auflage. *Martin Luther.* Göttingen: Vandenhoeck & Ruprecht, 1967. 382 pages.

7th revised edition, reprint from the German publication by Bernhard Lohse, *Martin Luther.* Berlin: Evanglische Verlagsanstalt, 1983. 369 pages. "Only for distribution in German Democratic Republic and in socialist foreign countries."

— *Martin Luther: Rebell für Glauben.* München: Wilhelm Heyne Verlag, 1983. 464 pages.

— Greek translation. [romanization] *Ed o steko mai: matinos Loutheros: he zoe tou, to ergon tou, he didaskalia tou.* Metaphrasis hypo Gerasimou Zerbopoulo. Athena: Logos, 1959. 368 pages.

— Italian translation. *Lutero.* Traduzione di Aldo Comba. Prefazione di Delio Cantimori. Torino: G. Einaudi 1960. 379 pages. Biblioteca di cultura storica, 65.

Traduzione di Aldo Comba. Milano: Edizione CDE Spa, 1960. 374 pages.

— Japanese translation. Tokyo: Japan NCC Literature Commission and Luthersha, 1954, n.p.

Reprinted. Tokyo: Seibunsha, n.d., n.p.

Korean translation. Seoul: Word of Life Press, 1982.

Second edition. *Maruť in Ruťo ui saengae.* Translated by Yi Chongťae omgim ui Malssumsa. 1996. 556 pages.

— Spanish translation. *Lutero.* Traducción de Raquel Lozada de Ayala Torales; revisada por A. F. Sosa. Buenos Aires: Editorial Sudamericana, 1955. 485 pages.

Second edition. Buenos Aires: Editorial Sudamericana; Mexico (D. F.): Edición Producida por Editorial Hermes, 1978. 485 pages.

Third edition. Mexido (D. F.): Ediciones CUPSA, 1989.

— Swedish translation. *Luther, Mannen som Blev en Epok.* Stockholm: Diakonistyrelsens Bokforlag, 1960. 359 pages.

— Chapter 21 was presented as an article, "Luther's Struggle for Faith" in *Festschrift für Gerhard Ritter zu seinem 60. Geburtstag,* published in 1950. See C8.

— Certain portions were taken in condensed form from the author's *The Martin Luther Christmas Book* published in 1948. See A10.

1951

A12   *The Travail of Religious Liberty: Nine Biographical Studies.* Philadelphia: Westminster, 1951. 272 pages.

This study gathers in one volume many aspects of intensive research undertaken by RHB in 1926 during his Guggenheim fellowship project. Much of the content of the work appeared in other forms in earlier publications. Written for the general public rather than the scholarly specialist, the contents of the book were originally presented in large part as the Sprunt Lectures at Union Theological Seminary in Richmond, Virginia in 1950. Portions were also delivered as lectures at the Danforth Conference, Camp Miniwanca, Shelly, Michigan; Eden Theological Seminary, Webster Groves, Missouri; and the Vermont Congregational Ministers' Conference, Montpelier, Vermont.

RHB uses a biographical approach to examine the problem of religious intolerance. He takes nine figures and treats them in three major sections. The first concerns Catholic and Protestant persecution, the second the Toleration Controversy of the sixteenth century, and the third the freedom of the individual in the seventeenth century up to the English Act of Toleration in 1689. Limited in scope to western Christendom in the late fifteenth through the seventeenth centuries, RHB's study presents the many forces at work making it difficult for religious tolerance to survive when religious truth is also sought. Some bibliography is provided with more complete documentation offered for new material presented in the last three chapters. The work is illustrated with line drawings by the author representing contemporary documents and art works.

— Paper edition. New York: Harper, 1958. 272 pages. Harper Torchbooks.

— Reprinted. Hamden, Ct: Archon Books, 1971. 272 pages.

— British edition. London: Lutterworth, 1953. 266 pages.

— Italian translation. *La Lotta per la libertà religiosa.* Traduzione di Franca Medioli Cavara. Bologna: Il Mulino, 1963. 263 pages. Saggi, 36.

2e ed, riveduta, da Francesco Lazzari. Bologna: Il Mulino, 1969. 281 pages. Saggi, 36.

4e ed. Bologna: Il Mulino, 1982. 268 pages. Universale paperbacks Il Mulino, 140.

1952

A13　*The Reformation of the Sixteenth Century.* Boston: Beacon, 1952. 276 pages.

This work is an example of RHB's interest in making the results of careful scholarship available to the general educated reader. It is a basic history of the Protestant Reformation focusing on religious aspects, a needed publication at the time it was written according to the author. Since its original publication, the work has been translated into many languages. The origins and development of the reform movement are presented as are the characteristic beliefs of Lutherans, Zwinglians, Catholics, and Anglicans. The book has a classified bibliography of English language titles and is indexed. Contemporary woodcuts provide illustrations some of which have been reinterpreted by RHB in line drawings.

— Reprinted, 1956 and 1959.

— Paper edition, 1952. Beacon Paperbacks.

— Boston: Beacon, 1960. 276 pages. Beacon Paperbacks.

— Boston: Beacon, 1968. 278 pages.

— Boston, Beacon, 1970. 278 pages. Beacon Paperbacks.

— Enlarged edition. With a foreword and supplementary bibliography by Jaroslav Pelikan. Boston: Beacon, 1985 c. 1952. 278 pages. Bibliography, pp. 262–70.

— British edition. London: Hodder and Stoughton, 1953. 276 pages.

Reprinted, 1957 and 1961.

New edition, 1963.

— 4th edition, 1965.

— Hebrew translation. Translated by Svi Rin. Tel Aviv: n.p., 1959. 199 pages.

Opening of *The Reformation of the Sixteenth Century* (A13). Courtesy Beacon Press.

— Indian translation. Telegu Theological Literature Board. Andhra Christian Council. Distributed by Prabodha Book Centre, Vijayawadam, n.d.

— Italian translation. *La Riforma protestante.* Traduzione di Francesco Lo Bue. Torino: Einaudi, 1958. 387 pages.

2e. ed. Prefazione di Delio Cantimori. Traduzione di Francesco Lo Bue. Torino: Einaudi, 1959. 387 pages. Piccola biblioteca Einaudi, 82.

Torino: Einaudi, 1966. 264 pages. Piccola biblioteca scientifico letteraria, 82.

Torino: Einaudi, 1971. 264 pages. Piccola Biblioteca Einaudi, 73.

— Japanese translation. Tokyo: Shinkyo Shuppansha, 1966. 307 pages.

— From British edition. Kobunda: Frontier Library, n.d. 217 pages.

— Korean edition. Translated by Young Il Seu. Seoul: Eun Seong, 1992. 326 pages.

1953

A14   *Hunted Heretic: The Life and Death of Michael Servetus 1511–1553.* Boston: Beacon, 1953. 270 pages.

This work is the last of RHB's major biographical studies of four Reformation figures martyred for the cause of religious liberty. It was completed twenty-five years after his original research began. Publication coincided with the four-hundredth anniversary of the burning of Michael Servetus. The contents of this work were delivered as the Tipple Lectures at Drew University in 1952.

Like the studies of Joris, Castellio, and Ochino, this volume was received upon publication as the definitive work on the subject. The work is appropriately dedicated to the members of RHB's extended family who were doctors. Servetus was a physician as well as having strong interests in biblical studies, linguistics, theology, and geography. His work on the circulation of the blood is well known. RHB takes a chronological approach to Servetus' life and carefully assesses the political, social, economic, and religious climate of the period. RHB's discussions of the doctrinal issues confronted by Servetus established the author as a theologian among some of the reviewers of this book.

— Paper edition, 1956. Beacon Paperbacks.

— New edition. With a new foreword by the author. Boston: Beacon, 1960. 270 pages. Beacon Series in Liberal Religion.

— Reprinted, 1964.

— Reprinted. Gloucester, Mass: Peter Smith, 1978. 270 pages.

— French edition. *Michel Servet; hérétique et martyr, 1511–1553.* Genève: E. Droz, 1953. 148 pages.

— Second edition. Issued a few months later with corrections. Travaux d'Humanisme et Renaissance, 6.

— German translation. *Michael Servet, 1511–1553.* Übersetzung von Senta Bergfield, Agnes Müller v. Brockhausen, und Gustav Adolf Benrath. Gütersloh: Gerd Mohn, 1960. 157 pages. Schriften des Vereins für Reformationsgeschichte, 178.

— Spanish translation. *Miguel Servet, el hereje perseguido (1511–1553).* Bibliografia de Servet par Madeline E. Stanton, Yale University. Traducción, prologo, bibliografia sobre Servet, por Angel Alcalá Galvez. Madrid: Ediciónes Taurus, 1973. 300 pages. Col. Ensayistas, 96.

— Chapter Two was elaborated and included under the title "Michael Servetus and the Trinitarian Speculation of the Middle Ages" in *Autour de Michel Servet et de Sébastien Castellion: Receuil,* published in 1953. See C11.

1954

A15   *The Covenant in the Wilderness: The New Haven Green in 1815.* New Haven: Yale University Press, 1954. 12 pages.

This pamphlet was "presented by the New Haven Association of Churches and Ministers to our friends attending the General Council of Congregational Christian Churches, June 23–30, 1954." Published by the printing office at the Yale University Press, it introduces the founding fathers of New Haven Colony and explains the establishment of the Congregational Church in New Haven by its Puritan forefathers.

Included are the beginnings of Yale. The events brought about by John Davenport and Theophilus Eaton are set in the larger context of the political and social circumstances in England and the New World that brought the new colony into being. A short summary of the growth of the community into the early nineteenth century is included. This exploration of local history, illustrated with line drawings by the author, is a delightful publication particularly for those with interest in the history of Yale or New Haven.

— Reprinted in *Collected Essays III*, pp. 227–38. See A29.

A15.5   *Roland Bainton Speaks on the Martin Luther Motion Picture.* New York: Lutheran Church Productions, Inc., 1954. 22 pages.

This short piece is an apology for Protestantism against Roman Catholic criticism in the form of explication of the "new" motion picture about Martin Luther. In his role as noted historian, RHB explained the historical facts behind the Reformation to an audience which apparently was afraid that the film was "unbiblical." The film was produced with the sponsorship and collaboration of the Lutheran Church in America "to set the record straight on Luther and the real religious issues of the Reformation" (p. 2). RHB spoke directly to the issue of religious liberty in his comments for this scholarly advertisement. The work includes artwork of the Reformation period portraying historical figures pictured next to photographs of the actors and actresses playing their parts in the film.

A16   *Friends in Relation to the Churches.* Guilford, N.C.: Guilford College, 1954. 16 pages.

Delivered as the 1954 Ward Lecture at Guilford College, this short work reflects RHB's concern for both the Quakers and other denominations as they responded to the then recent organization of the World Council of Churches in 1948. It is persuasive and rhetorical in character aimed at an academic audience. Although there are footnotes, there are no table of contents, bibliography, index, or illustrative material.

— Published as an article in *Inward Light*, 21:55 (Spring, 1958): 29–40. See D137.

1956

A17   *The Age of the Reformation.* Princeton, N.J.: Van Nostrand, 1956. 192
       pages. An Anvil Original.

The first of RHB's three works written for the Anvil series, this title is
dedicated to the author's graduate students with doctorates in Reformation studies. It follows the series format with two major sections. The
first presents an historical account of the Age of the Reformation look-
ing at denominational concerns, geographical factors, political aspects,
and effects of the Reformation. RHB tries to show that "the religious
revolution of the sixteenth century shattered an ecclesiastical structure
and quickened a universal faith." The second section presents support-
ing documents selected and translated into English to illustrate the text.
In his introduction, RHB notes the difficulty of using abridged primary
sources. A brief bibliography and index are included. The work is not
illustrated.

— Reprint edition. Malabar, Fla.: Krieger, 1984. 191 pages.

1957

A18   *What Christianity Says about Sex, Love, and Marriage.* New York: Associa-
       tion Press, 1957. 124 pages. An Association Press Reflection Book.

A small book directed to a popular audience, this title is arranged in five
chapters. RHB treats his topic historically presenting the Church's views
on sex, love, and marriage in the periods of the Roman Empire, the
Middle Ages, the Reformation, and the Modern Period. An earlier
chapter explains the fundamental precepts of the Christian Church on
these questions. Brief footnotes and bibliography are included.

— British edition. *Sex, Love, and Marriage: A Christian Survey.* London and Glasgow: Collins, 1958. 128 pages. Fontana Books.

— Reprinted, 1962.

— This work was originally published as an article under the title of
"Christianity and Sex: An Historical Survey" in *Pastoral Psychology* 3:26
(September, 1952): 10–26, 4:21; (February, 1953): 12–29.

— This work also appeared earlier under the title "Christianity and
Sex: An Historical Survey" in *Sex and Religion Today* edited by Simon
Doniger and published in 1953. See C55.

A19   *Vignettes of Men Memorialized in the Buildings of the Yale Divinity School,* with drawings by the author. New Haven: Yale Divinity School, 1957. 13 pages.

Condensed from the author's *Yale and the Ministry,* this short pamphlet presents brief sketches in narrative form of figures important in the history of Yale Divinity School from Leonard Bacon (1802–1882) to Frank Chamberlain Porter (1859–1946). RHB has illustrated this work with line drawings throughout, and a sketch of the Sterling Divinity Quadrangle is found on the cover. A map of the Divinity School concludes the work.

A20   *Yale and the Ministry; A History of Education for the Christian Ministry at Yale from the Founding in 1701.* New York: Harper, 1957. 297 pages.

Dedicated to RHB's colleagues at Yale Divinity School, particularly Robert C. Calhoun, H. Richard Niebuhr, and Paul Vieth, this work examines the role of Yale in the history of religious thought and ministry of Connecticut and the nation as a whole. "The grand errand" of the founding fathers of New Haven "to propagate the blessed Protestant religion in the wilderness" is traced historically from 1702 to 1957. The changing patterns of and approaches to theology, piety, and social reform at Yale are presented. RHB has provided extensive bibliographical and archival references although there is no formal bibliography. The book is illustrated with line drawings and sketches by the author as well as with photographs. Those Yale alumni who have enjoyed RHB's talks on the history of Yale Divinity School will find this book of interest.

— 1985 edition. San Francisco: Harper & Row. 311 pages. "Epilogue" copyright by Leander Keck, pp. 269–81.

1958

A21   *Pilgrim Parson: The Life of James Herbert Bainton, 1867–1942.* New York: Nelson, 1958. 166 pages.

Dedicated to RHB's sister Hilda, this volume presents a biography of the author's father with whom he had a close and affectionate relationship. James Herbert Bainton was a Congregational pastor serving parishes first in England, then British Columbia and Washington state, and finally Connecticut. The book addresses issues of concern in Congregational circles but emphasizes the senior Bainton's non-parochial view of life in which he was "a pilgrim in search of the essentials of his faith." The book is illustrated with the pen and ink sketches and line drawings, which have delighted many of the author's students, friends, and acquaintances. A photograph of his father serves as a frontispiece. The book is directed to a general audience and there are no footnotes, bibliography, or index.

1959

A21.5   *The Douglas Clyde Macintosh Fellowship in Theology and the Philosophy of Religion Established in honor of her husband by Hope Conklin Macintosh in the Year of Our Lord Nineteen Hundred and Fifty-nine.* New Haven, Ct.: 1959. 12 pages. Cover illustration by RHB.

In this pamphlet, RHB honored his colleague at Yale Divinity School as well as Mrs. Macintosh who was also an educator and historian. A note at the end refers the reader to *Yale and the Ministry* (see A20) for "a fuller account of the place of Douglas Macintosh in the succession of New England's theologians."

1960

A22   *Christian Attitudes toward War and Peace: An Historical Survey and Critical Re-evaluation.* New York: Abingdon, 1960. 299 pages. Apex Books.

This exhaustive sweep over the history of the Church on questions of war and peace was acclaimed as a significant publication when it was published. Speaking directly to the pressing problems of life and death in the atomic age, RHB brought his own passionate concern with peace into this historical study of the Christian response to war. He saw three attitudes recurring throughout history in the Christian ethical response to the Gospel; pacifism, the just war, and the crusade. These themes are examined chronologically from the classical era, Old and New Testament times, the Roman Empire, to the modern era. RHB took a close look at the peace churches. His own opinions are offered at the end of the book. The work has extensive bibliographical references, although there is no formal bibliography, and it is addressed to the general educated reader.

RHB noted in this book that it was thirty years in the making. Portions were given earlier as lectures. Beginning sections were presented as the Ayer Lectures at Rochester Theological Seminary in 1939. The Cromwellian materials were given as the Southworth Lectures at Andover-Newton Theological Seminary in 1943. The survey as a whole was given as the Kerr Lectures at the Divinity School, McMaster University in 1958. Sketches of the whole were offered at the Washington Conference of Methodist Ministers as well as the New York Conference of Methodist Ministers in 1959.

— Republished. Nashville: Abingdon, 1978. 299 pages.

— Paperback. Nashville: Abingdon, 1979.

— British edition. London: Hodder and Stoughton, 1961. 299 pages.

— Italian translation. *Il Cristiano, la guerra, la pace rassegna storica e valutazione critica*. Traduzione di Lina e Mario Miegge. Torino: Gribaudi, 1968. 348 pages. Critical/critica, 4.

— This translation contains a unique supplement published only in the Italian edition. The original English manuscript has the heading "The Ethics of Peace: Peace and War in Recent Pronouncements of Catholic Leaders."

— Japanese translation. Translated by Toeko Nakomura. Tokyo: Shinkyo Shuppansha, 1963. 357 pages.

— Spanish translation. *Actitudes cristianas ante la guerra y la paz; examen histórico y nueva valoración critica*. Traducción de Rafael Muñoz-Rojas. Madrid: Editorial Tecnos, 1963. 247 pages. Semilla y Surco. Collección de ciencas sociales, 27.

— Part of the original work was excerpted and published under the title "From Outlawry of War to A-Bomb." *Christian Century*, 77:39 (28 September 1960): 1112–15.

A23   *Early Christianity*. Princeton, N.J.: Van Nostrand, 1960. 192 pages. An Anvil Original.

One of three Anvil series publications written by RHB this work covers the history of early Christianity in four sections: "The Rise of Christianity," "The Church in the Age of Persecution," "The Church and Society," and "The Christian Roman Empire." The work is aimed at the beginning student of this historical period. A second section of documents and readings includes selected primary sources in English translation to illustrate and supplement historical narrative presented in the first section. A basic bibliography, a chronological table of events and historical figures, and an index are provided. The book is not illustrated.

— Republished. Princeton, N.J.: Van Nostrand, 1969.

— Reprinted. Malabar, Fla: Krieger, 1984. 187 pages.

— Microfilmed. Gainesville, Florida: George A. Smathers Libraries Preservation Department, University of Florida, 1994 c. 1969.

1961

A24   *El Alma hispana y el alma sajona.* Buenos Aires: Editorial "La Aurora," 1961. 142 pages. Catedra Carnahan.

— Published only in Spanish, this title was written in English as lectures and delivered by RHB during a South American tour. Lectures included are "The Spanish and the Saxon Soul," "No Spanish Type," "The Spanish Ecclesiastical Type," "Tolerance toward Heresy," "Tolerance as to Paganism," and "Tolerance as to Race." The volume ends with the author's conclusions. Bibliographical footnotes are provided.

— The English version of the lectures are part of the Roland H. Bainton Papers. Listed on p. 27 of the Register. See R1.

1962

A25   *The Medieval Church.* Princeton, N.J.: Van Nostrand, 1962. 191 pages. An Anvil Original.

The last of RHB's contributions to the Anvil series, this volume traces the role of the church in the development of religious, intellectual, and institutional life from A.D. 400 to 1500. It follows the format of the series presenting an early section of historical narrative on the major movements of church history. The latter section presents related primary source materials translated into English. A bibliography arranged by major topical areas, a brief chronology of events, and an index are provided. There are no illustrations.

— Revised edition, 1963.

— Reprinted. Huntington, N.Y.: Krieger, 1979. 191 pages.

— Reprinted. Melbourne: Krieger, 1979. Paperback, 192 pages.

— Reprinted. Malabar, Fla: Krieger, 1983. 191 pages.

— Reprinted. Malabar, Fla: Krieger, 1985. 191 pages.

A26   *Collected Papers in Church History: Series One; Early and Medieval Christianity.* Boston: Beacon, 1962. 261 pages.

The first of three volumes gathering together RHB's shorter writings for the general reader, *Early and Medieval Christianity* presents articles in three areas of concern: "Patristic and Medieval History," "Continuities and Changes from Medieval to Renaissance Christianity," and "Religion and the Church in the Renaissance." It reflects RHB's early career in the history of the Early Church and demonstrates his wide range of scholarly interests together with the two subsequent volumes. All but one article in Series One was published earlier in sources that are indicated. A selected bibliography of RHB's writings from 1922 to 1961 is found at the end of the work, and an index is provided.

— British edition. London: Hodder and Stoughton, 1965. 261 pages.

— See also A1.

A27   *Luther's Meditations on the Gospels.* Translated and arranged by Roland H. Bainton. Illustrated with woodcuts by Virgil Solis. Philadelphia: Westminster, 1962. 155 pages.

Excerpted, translated, and arranged by RHB from Luther's sermons and letters, this small work is amply and appealingly illustrated with woodcuts by Virgil Solis published originally in 1562 in Viet Dietrich's epitome of Luther's Bible. RHB attempted to select "the piquant, poignant, profound, and comprehensive" passages for inclusion in his book to make Luther's thought alive for contemporary folk. Sources for the passages are included in the back with references to the Weimar edition of Luther's works. The book is dedicated to Heinrich Bornkamm "who has so greatly enriched our understanding of the Bible."

— British edition, 1963.

1963

A28   *Collected Papers in Church History: Series Two: Studies on the Reformation.* Boston: Beacon, 1963. 289 pages.

The second of three volumes collecting shorter writings of RHB, this work represents the author's primary scholarly concern with studies in the Reformation. It is presented in a form useful to the general educated reader and beginning student of the period. Essays are divided into three main sections: "Martin Luther and the Reformation." "The Left Wing of the Reformation," and "Religious Struggles after the Reformation." A selected bibliography of RHB's writings is provided as well as an index. The book is illustrated with examples of contemporary woodcuts, portraits, paintings, and engravings.

— Paper edition, 1966.

— *British* edition. London: Hodder and Stoughton, 1964. 289 pages.

— Canadian edition. Toronto: Saunders, 1963. 289 pages.

1964

A29   *Collected Papers in Church History: Series Three; Christian Unity and Religion in New England.* Boston: Beacon, 1964. 294 pages.

This third volume of collected papers of RHB contains an expression of thanks to the Beacon Press for publishing the series evidencing "a concern for scholarship rather than a quest for affluence." While reflecting the author's careful scholarship, the collection of articles in *Series Three* is in useful form for the general educated reader and beginning student. The first three sections contain articles concerned with the problems of reunion of the churches. They are entitled "The Unity of Man and the Unity of the Church," "Church Unity and the Denominations," and "The Church and Society." The final section concerns the religious history of New England. A bibliography of RHB's works from 1919 to 1963 is found at the end of the work and an index is provided.

— British edition. London: Hodder and Stoughton, 1964. 294 pages.

— See also A15.

A30   *The Horizon History of Christianity.* New York: American Heritage; book trade distribution by Harper & Row, 1964. 432 pages.

RHB wrote the narrative portion of this large book, which was later reworked for the editions entitled *Christendom* and *The Penguin History of Christianity.* The original edition is generously illustrated with color photographs of artistic and historic artifacts representing the history of

Christianity. The author chronologically traced Christian history in word and picture from "The Ministry of Christ" to "Christianity in the Modern Age." Directed to the general reader, the work does not have full bibliographical apparatus. *Christendom* is more suitable for academic study and has black and white instead of color illustrations.

— Paper edition. New York: Avon Books, 1966. 430 pages.

— British edition. *The History of Christianity.* London: Nelson, 1964. 432 pages.

— Reprinted British edition. *The History of Christianity.* London: Reprint Society, 1966. 432 pages.

— "Reprinted, revised, and expanded" edition. *Christendom: A Short History of Christianity and its Impact on Western Civilization.* New York: Harper & Row, 1966. 2 volumes: *From the Birth of Christ to the Reformation* and *From the Reformation to the Present.* Harper Torchbooks. The Cloister Library.

— "Reprinted, revised, expanded" edition. *Christendom: A Short History of Christianity.* Harper Colophon Books

— British edition. *The Penguin History of Christianity.* 2 vols. Harmondsworth: Penguin, 1967.

— Swiss edition (in French). *Notre Église à deux mille ans.* Translated by A. Péry. Genève: Labor et Fides, 1969. 224 pages.

— Later paperback edition. *Christianity.* (originally published as *The Horizon History of Christianity*). Boston: American Heritage, 1985. 416 pages. The American Heritage Library.

1969

A31   *Erasmus of Christendom.* New York: Scribner, 1969. 308 pages.

Written fifteen years after RHB's major study of Martin Luther, this work on Erasmus is an expansion of the five Stone Lectures delivered at Princeton in 1967. A briefer version was presented as the Menno Simons Lectures at Bethel College, North Newton, Kansas. Attracted by Erasmus' spiritual religion derived from the Brethren of the Common Life, his moderation and toleration, and his hatred of war, RHB presents a thoroughly documented study written for the general educated public. In his autobiography, RHB commented that "the 'Erasmus' was done while student unrest was rampant and disorganizing the universities, and the proper word then was 'Come now, let us reason together.'" (*Roly,* p. 193. See A39) The book was acclaimed upon publication and continues to be an important source on Erasmus and his times. Its popular appeal is evidenced by its translation into numerous languages and the reviews which have appeared in countless newspapers and journals.

While essentially a biographical study of Erasmus, social, economic, intellectual, political, and religious questions of the early reform period are carefully elaborated. The work is heavily illustrated with black and white representations from contemporary woodcuts, portraits, paintings, sketches, and maps. Footnotes are provided after each chapter. An extensive bibliography is found at the end of the volume, which indicates English translations of Erasmus' writings, critical editions of his works, bibliographies relating to Erasmus, and secondary works on the subject. An index is provided.

— Paper edition with corrections, 1969.

— Hardcover edition. New York: Scribner, 1977 c. 1969. 308 pages.

— Paper edition. New York: Crossroad, 1982 c. 1969. 308 pages.

— British edition. London: Collins, 1972 c. 1969. 399 pages. Fontana Library of Theology and Philosophy.

— Paper edition. London: Lion, 1996.

— Canadian edition. Toronto: Macmillan, 1969. 299 pages.

— Don Mills, Ontario: Saunders, 1969. 320 pages.

— German translation. *Erasmus: Reformer zwischen den Fronten.* Berechtigte übersetzung aus dem Amerikanischen von Elisabeth Langerbeck. Göttingen: Vandenhoeck & Ruprecht, 1972. 301 pages.

— Italian translation. *Erasmo della Cristianità.* Introd. di Antonio Rotondò. Trad. di Albano Biondi. Firenze: Sansoni, 1970. 337 pages.

— Japanese translation. Translated by Akira Demura. Tokyo: United Church of Christ in Japan, 1971. 410 pages.

1971

A32   *Women of the Reformation in Germany and Italy.* Minneapolis: Augsburg, 1971. 279 pages.

The first of a trilogy on women of the Reformation, this book is yet another example of RHB's concern with giving "those who haven't had their due some historical attention." RHB based his work on extensive scholarly research although the book was written for the general reading public. RHB responded to contemporary interest in women's studies in his choice of topic, but it must be remembered that he had addressed the questions of women's roles in religious circles in earlier books and articles. An example is his 1955 Dudlein Lecture at Harvard entitled "The Role of the Minister's Wife in New England."

Using a biographical approach, the author examined nine German women and six Italian women who played prominent roles in both Protestant and Catholic reform movements during the sixteenth century. Other themes addressed are the manner in which reform thought was disseminated and the impact of the Reformation on the social order particularly the role of women in the Church. Each figure is placed in the context of political and social events of the era. Bibliographical references follow each study and illustrative material includes contemporary portraits, drawings, woodcuts, and engravings. Maps are included.

— Paper edition. Boston: Beacon, 1974. 279 pages. Beacon Paperbacks.

— Italian edition. *Donne della Riforma in Germania, in Italia e in Francia.* Trad. di Flavio Sarni. Introduzione "Per una storia delle donne nella Reforma," di Susanna Peryonel Rambaldi. Torino: Claudiana, 1992. 460 pages. May include part of A33.

— German edition. *Frauen der Reformation: von Katharine von Bora bis Anna Zwingli: 10 Porträts.* Aus dem Englischen übersetzt und bearbeitet von Marion Obitz. Gütersloher Verlagshaus, 1995. 191 pages.

1973

A33   *Women of the Reformation in France and England.* Minneapolis: Augsburg 1973. 287 pages.

This second volume in RHB's studies of women of the Reformation presents sketches of five French women and nine English women. The author stated that he did not pursue his earlier thesis that the end of monasticism in Protestant territories exalted the status of women at home as he had in his first book. Rather he surmised that "the individualization of faith" made for "the personalization of marriage." His research indicated that the religious concerns and commitment of women had become important in decisions of marriage.

This book exhibits RHB's scholarly diligence in areas where sources were lacking. The book was written in a style intended for the general reading public. A brief bibliography and notes follow each section. The book is illustrated with contemporary portraits, woodcuts, drawings, and engravings. An index and a guide to the sources of illustrations are provided.

— Reprinted paper edition. Boston, Beacon, 1975, c. 1973. 287 pages.

1974

A34   *Behold the Christ.* Assisted by Sumathi Devasahayam. New York: Harper & Row, 1974. 224 pages.

This heavily illustrated volume explores the artistic responses of various cultures to the story of Jesus throughout the history of Christianity. RHB collected many black and white photographs of drawings, paintings, and sculpture and contributed his own line drawings to illustrate the historical narrative of the book. Clearly and simply written, the work is directed to a popular audience and bears witness to the author's lifelong interest in Christian art. Following an introduction, the work is organized around episodes in the life of Christ and is arranged chronologically within each section presenting examples from the early churches up to the present day. A selected bibliography by period and topic is provided as well as a list of sources used for illustration. In his autobiography, RHB noted that the Catholic Book Club adopted this book as one of its selections.

— Paper edition, 1976.

1977

A35   *Women of the Reformation from Spain to Scandinavia.* Minneapolis: Augsburg Publishing House, 1977. 240 pages.

The last of RHB's three studies of women of the Reformation, this work examines twenty-seven women of the Reformation from Spain, Portugal, Scotland, England, Denmark, Norway, Sweden, Poland, Hungary, and Transylvania. RHB acknowledges the linguistic assistance of a number of people as the scope of the work involves numerous languages and a wide range of materials.

Questions addressed include the role of women in administrative and religious circles and the status of women and marriage. RHB indicated that he wished to correct historical distortion, which suggested that women were enslaved during this period. Written for a general audience, this work offers short bibliographies after each section. It is illustrated with black and white line drawings, portraits, and engravings from the period. An index and a guide to the sources for illustrations are also included.

1978

A36   *Yesterday, Today, and What Next?; Reflections on History and Hope.* Minneapolis: Augsburg, 1978. 141 pages.

Written as a preliminary reflection to be followed by his autobiography, this book reveals much of the author's personal outlook on history. Themes addressed are the nature of history and the character of the discipline, the special outlook of Christian history, and the message of the past to the present as the modern age faces frightening dilemmas. His chapter entitled "Today and What Next?" reminds the reader of RHB's lifelong concern with questions of peace and war and the place of pacifism amid the realities of historical necessity. The author emphasizes the value of history for understanding human nature. A selected bibliography on several topics is included at the end. A color reproduction of Bainton's portrait painted by Deane Keller for the Yale Divinity School is found on the front cover.

— Korean translation. *Yoksa wa huimang.* Translated by Kim Sangsinyhok. Soul T'ukpyolsi: Taehan Kidokkyo Sohoe, 1980. 194 pages. 1983. Hyondae sinso, 110.

A37   *The Martin Luther Easter Book.* Translated and arranged by Roland H. Bainton. Illustrated and with woodcuts by Virgil Solis. Philadelphia: Fortress, 1983. 87 pages.

This volume's text is taken from Luther's *Meditations on the Gospels*, translated and arranged by Roland Bainton in 1962 (see A27 and B6). Translation was done from the Weimar edition of Luther's works with assistance from the Erwin Mulhaupt five-volume edition of Luther's sermons on the Gospels. Passages were selected as sources of inspiration expressing "the piquant, the poignant, and the profound" on the subjects of the journey to Jerusalem and Holy Week, the Lord's Supper, Jesus' arrest and trial, the Crucifixion, and the Resurrection.

The woodcuts were taken from a replica of Luther's Bible published by Viet Dietrich, his associate, in Frankfurt in 1562 under the title *Summaria*. They are important in the history of gospel iconography because the artist identified himself in his work. Solis (1514–62) was a resident of Nuremberg. Roland Bainton used bracketed text to indicate his own remarks and summaries apart from the texts of Luther. The book includes an introduction and was published with a paper cover.

— See also B8.

A38   *A Pilgrimage to Luther's Germany* with Herbert Brokering and Roland Bainton. Minneapolis: Winston, 1983. 79 pages.

Published as an inspirational book for a popular audience, this volume records the essence of Roland Bainton's pilgrimage to the eastern German sites that were important in the life and history of Martin Luther. Bainton died the following year. Printed on glossy paper, the book is filled with appealing and colorful photographs of everyday scenes from modern German life, works of art, and significant places such as the cities of Wittenberg and Heidelberg, Wartburg Castle, and the Augustinian Cloister in Erfurt. On the lower left-hand pages are quotations from Bainton's *Here I Stand* (see A11, 1978 edition). The pages on the right-hand side include quotations from Luther and poetry and prose written by Bainton and Herbert Brokering relating to Christian theology in the spirit of Luther. The volume includes a foreword by Herbert Brokering who accompanied Bainton on this trip as well as a list of photo credits. There is no table of contents or index.

1988

A39   *Roly: Chronicle of a Stubborn Non-Conformist.* Edited by Ruth C. L.
      Gritsch. New Haven: Yale Divinity School, 1988. 216 pages.

These memoirs, written by Roland H. Bainton not long before his
death in 1984, were published in 1988 by Yale Divinity School in con-
junction with the creation of the Roland H. Bainton Fund, which
brings to the Yale campus people associated with church history and
issues of peace with justice. The publication was condensed from the
much longer original manuscript and also edited by Ruth Gritsch with
the assistance of the Bainton family, according to the foreword to the
book by Leander E. Keck, dean of Yale Divinity School in 1988. Bainton shared his life with his readers in conversational and reminiscing
style within twenty-one chronologically arranged chapters. References
to the works listed in this bibliography and the subjects and authors it
includes are frequent in *Roly*. It is not indexed however. Bainton's
sketches serve as illustrations.

B. TRANSLATIONS BY RHB

1935

B1   Castellio, Sebastian. *Concerning Heretics.* New York: Columbia University Press, 1935. 342 pages. Records of Civilization: Sources and Studies, no. 22.

— For further information see A4.

1937

B2   Holborn, Hajo. *Ulrich von Hutten and the German Reformation.* Translated by Roland H. Bainton. New Haven: Yale University Press and London: H. Milford, Oxford University Press, 1937. 214 pages. Yale Historical Publications: Studies, 11.

— Published under the direction of the Department of History on the Kingsley Trust Association Publication Fund established by the Scroll and Key Society of Yale College.

— Reprinted. Westport, Ct.: Greenwood, 1978. 219 pages. Yale Historical Publications Series, No. 11.

— British edition. London: Oxford University Press, 1937.

1948

B3   Luther, Martin. *The Martin Luther Christmas Book.* Philadelphia: Westminster, 1948. 74 pages.

— For further information see A10.

1953

B4   Gedat, Gustav-Adolf. *They Built for Eternity.* Translated by Roland H. Bainton. Nashville and New York: Abingdon-Cokesbury, 1953. 175 pages.

— Reprinted. North Stratford: Ayer, 1977. Essay Index Reprint Series.

1960

B5   Dörries, Hermann. *Constantine and Religious Liberty.* Translated by Roland H. Bainton. New Haven: Yale University Press, 1960. 141 pages. Terry Lecture Series, 1958–59.

1962

B6   Luther, Martin. *Meditations on the Gospels.* Philadelphia: Westminster, 1962. 74 pages.

— For further information see A27.

1972

B7   Dörries, Hermann, *Constantine the Great.* Translated by Roland H. Bainton. New York: Harper and Row, 1972. 250 pages. Harper Torchbooks.

1983

B8   Luther, Martin. *The Martin Luther Easter Book.* Philadelphia: Fortress, 1983. 87 pages,

— For further information see A37.

C. ARTICLES PUBLISHED IN MONOGRAPHS

Studies in Church History

1922

C1   "Church History and Progress." In *Education for Christian Service*, 243–66, by members of the faculty of the Divinity School of Yale University in commemoration of its 100th anniversary. New Haven: Yale University Press, 1922.

1931

C2   "Sebastian Castellio and the Toleration Controversy of the Sixteenth Century." In *Persecution and Liberty: Essays in Honor of George Lincoln Burr*, 183–209. New York: Century, 1931.

— Reprinted. Freeport, N.Y.: Books for Libraries Press, 1968.

1938

C3   "The Appeal to Reason and the American Constitution." In *The Constitution Reconsidered*, 121–30. Edited for the American Historical Association by Conyers Read. New York: Columbia University Press, 1938.

— Revised edition with a new preface by Richard B. Morris, 121–30. New York: Harper and Row, 1968. Harper Torchbooks.

— Reprinted in *Collected Papers III*, 201–11. See A29.

1940

C4   "The Congregational Idea of the Church." In *The Witness of the Churches of the Congregational Order: Papers Exchanged by Baptists, Congregational-Christians, and Disciples in 1940*, 35–42. Edited by Harlan Paul Douglass. New York: Northern Baptist Convention, 1940.

1945

C5   "The Unity of Mankind in the Classical Christian Tradition." In *The Albert Schweitzer Jubilee Book*, 277–96. Edited by A. A. Roback. Cambridge, Mass.: Sci-Art, 1945.

— Reprinted in *Collected Papers III*, 3–23. See A29.

— Reprinted. Westport, Ct.: Greenwood, 1970.

1948

C6   "The Early Church and War." In *The Church, the Gospel, and War,* 75–92. Edited by Rufus M. Jones. New York: Harper, 1948.

— Reprinted. New York: Garland, 1971. The Garland Library of War and Peace.

— Reprinted in *Christian Life: Ethics, Morality, and Discipline in the Early Church.* New York: Garland, 1993. Studies in Early Christianity, v. 16.

— First published in *Harvard Theological Review* 39 (July 1946): 189–212.

— German translation. "Die frühe Kirche und der Krieg." In *Das frühe Christentum in römischen Staat,* 187–216. Compiled by Richard Klein. Darmstadt: Wissenschaftliches Buchgesellschaft, 1971. Wege der Forschung, 267.

1949

C7   "The Puritan Theocracy and the Cambridge Platform." In *The Cambridge Platform of 1648: Tercentenary Commemoration at Cambridge, Massachusetts, October 27,1948,* 76–86. Arranged by the Joint Commission of the Congregational Christian Churches of the United States and the American Unitarian Association. Boston: Beacon Press for the Joint Commission, 1949.

— Also published in *The Minister's Quarterly* 6 (February 1949): 16–21.

— Reprinted in *Collected Papers III,* 215–26. See A29.

1950

C8   "Luther's Struggle for Faith." In *Festschrift für Gerhard Ritter zu seinem 60. Geburtstag,* 232–43. Hrsg. von Richard Nürnberger. Tübingen: J.C.B. Mohr, 1950.

— First published in *Church History,* 17 (September 1948): 193–206.

— Also published in *The Reformation: Material or Spiritual?*, 92–99. Edited by Lewis W. Spitz. Boston: Heath, 1962. Problems in European Civilization.

— Also published in *The Reformation: Basic Interpretations*. Edited and with introduction by Lewis W. Spitz. Lexington, Mass.: Heath, 1972. Problems in European Civilization.

— Reprinted in *Collected Papers II*, 14–19. See A28.

— This article became chapter 21 of *Here I Stand* (See A11). 1951.

C9   "Sebastian Castellio, Champion of Religious Liberty, 1515–1563." In *Castellioniana: Quatre Études sur Sébastien Castellion et l'idée de la tolérance*, 25–79, par Roland H. Bainton, Bruno Becker, Marius Valkhoff et Sape van der Woude. Le comité hollandaise pour la commémoration de Servet et de Castellion. Leiden: Brill, 1951.

— Reprinted in *Collected Papers II*, 139–84. See A28.

— Also published. Genève: Labor et Fides, 1964.

1953

C10   "Man, God and the Church in the Age of the Renaissance." In *The Renaissance: A Symposium,* 41–62a. New York: Metropolitan Museum of Art, 1953.

— An abstract of the projected speech by RHB for the Symposium is found in *Renaissance News* 5 (spring 1952): 8–10. The original article was entitled "The Thirst for God in the Renaissance."

— Published later in *The Journal of Religious Thought* 11 (spring/summer 1954): 119–33.

— Also published in *The Renaissance: Six Essays*, 77–96, by Walter K. Ferguson et al. New York: Harper and Row, 1962. Harper Torchbooks. The Academy Library.

— Reprinted in *Collected Papers I*, 185–203. See A26.

C11   "Michael Servetus and the Trinitarian Speculation of the Middle Ages." In *Autour de Michel Servet et de Sébastien Castellion: Receuil*, 29–46. Edited by Bruno Becker. Haarlem: H. D. Tjeenk Willink, 1953.

— This article is an elaboration of chapter 2 of *Hunted Heretic* (A14).

— Reprinted in *Collected Papers I,* 185–203. See A26.

1955

C12   "Patristic Christianity." In *The Idea of History in the Ancient Near East,* 215–36. Edited by Robert Claude Dentan. New Haven: Yale University Press and London: Oxford University Press, 1955. American Oriental Series, v. 38.

— Reprinted. New Haven: Yale University Press, 1967. 376 pages. Lectures of the Department of Near Eastern Languages and Literature at Yale University. Yale paperbound.

— Reprinted. New Haven: American Oriental Society, 1983. 376 pages. Lectures of the Department of Near Eastern Languages and Literature at Yale University.

1956

C13   "The Ministry in the Middle Ages." In *The Ministry in Historical Perspectives,* 82–109. Edited by H. Richard Niebuhr and Daniel D. Williams. New York: Harper, 1956.

— Reprinted in *Collected Papers I,* 45–80. See A26.

1957

C14   "The Anabaptist Contribution to History." In *The Recovery of the Anabaptist Vision: A Sixtieth Anniversary Tribute to Harold Bender,* 317–26. Edited by Guy F. Hershberger. Scottdale, Pa.: Herald Press, 1957.

— Reprinted in *Collected Papers I,* 199–207. See A28.

— German translation. "Die täuferische Beitrag zur Geschichte." In *Das Täufertum; Erbe und Verpflichtung,* 299–308. Stuttgart: Evangelisches Verlagswerk, 1963. Die Kirchen der Welt, Reihe B, 2.

C15   "Luther's Simple Faith." In *Luther Today,* 3–33, by Roland H. Bainton, Warren A. Quanbeck, and E. Gordon Rupp. Decorah, Ia.: Luther College Press, 1957.

— Reviewed by Edwin P. Booth in *Religion in Life,* 27:632–33.

C15.5   "Luther's Use of Direct Discourse." In *Luther Today,* 13. Decorah, Ia.: Luther College Press, 1957. Martin Luther Lectures, v. 1.

C15.6　"The Aarhus Conference." In *Luther Today.* See C15.5, 27.

1958

C16　"Probleme der Lutherbiographie." In *Lutherforschung Heute Referate und Berichte des 1. Internationalen Lutherforschungskongresses,* 24–31. Aarhus, 18.–23. August 1956. Hrsg. von Vilmos Vajta. Berlin: Lutherisches Verlagshaus, 1958.

— Published in English under the title "Problems in Luther Biography." In *Collected Papers II*, 92–103. See A28.

1960

C17　"Alexander Campbell and Church Unity." In *The Sage of Bethany: A Pioneer in Broadcloth*, 81–94. Compiled by Perry Epler Gresham. St. Louis: Bethany Press, 1960.

— Mimeographed copy. Bethany, West Virginia: Bethany College, 1956. 10 leaves. The Second Orem E. Scott Lectures, Bethany College, 4 April 1956.

— Reprinted under the title "The Disciples: Alexander Campbell and Church Unity." In *Collected Papers III*, 89–99.

— Also published as an article in *Ecumenical Studies Series*, 1957. See D58.

"Alexander Campbell and the Social Order." In *The Sage of Bethany*, 117–29.

— Both articles also appear in *The Sage of Bethany*. Joplin, Mo.: College Press, 1988. 189 pages.

C18　"The Bible and the Reformation." In *Five Essays on the Bible: Papers Read at the 1960 Annual Meeting* (of the American Council of Learned Societies Devoted to Humanistic Studies), 2–29. New York: The American Council of Learned Societies, 1960.

— Reprinted in *Collected Papers II*, 3–12. See A28.

1961

C19   "The Reformation." In *Chapters in Western Civilization,* 336–80. Third Edition. Edited by the Contemporary Civilization Staff of Columbia College, Columbia University. New York: Columbia University Press, 1961.

C19.5 "Renaissance and Religion." In *Die Religion in Geschichte und Gegenwart,* 5:159–63. 6 volumes. Tübingen: Mohr, 1961.

1962

C20   "The Cultivated Man and the Christian Man: Petrarch, St. Francis, and Albert Schweitzer." In *Albert Schweitzer's Realms: A Symposium,* 339–57. Edited by Abraham Aaron Roback. Cambridge, Mass.: Sci-Art, 1962.

— Reprinted. Westport, Ct.: Greenwood, 1970.

C21   "Interpretations of the Reformation." *The Reformation: Material or Spiritual?,* 1–7. Edited by Lewis W. Spitz. Boston: Heath, 1962. Problems in European Civilization.

— For further information see D61.

— For other RHB articles in this publication see C8.

C22   "Die Ursprünge des Epiphaniasfestes." In *Bild und Verkündigung: Festgabe für Hanna Jursch zum 60. Geburtstag,* 9–20. Berlin: Evangelische Verlagsanstalt, 1962. RHB article translated by Ilse Jursch. The English version of this article, "The Origins of Epiphany," was included in *Worship in Early Christianity.* New York: Garland, 1993. Studies in Early Christianity, vol. 16.

1963

C23   "The Bible in the Reformation." In *The Cambridge History of the Bible: The West from the Reformation to the Present Day,* 3:1–37. Edited by S. C. Greenslade. Cambridge: Cambridge University Press, 1963–70.

— Paper edition, 1975.

1965

C24   "Four Reviews." In *Italian Reformation Studies in Honor of Laelius Socinus,* 1–9. Edited by John A. Tedeschi. Firenze: Monnier, 1965. Università di Siena, Facoltà di Giurisprudenza, Collana di studi Pietro Rossi, n.s, vol. 4.

1967

C25   "Erasmus and Luther and the Dialog Julius Exclusus." In *Vierhundertfünf-zig Jahre Lutherische Reformation 1517–1967, Festschrift für Franz Lau zum 60. Geburtstag*, 17–26. Göttingen: Vandenhoeck & Ruprecht, 1967.

C26   "Erasmus and the Wesen des Christentums." In *Glaube, Geist, Geschichte; Festschrift für Ernst Benz zum 60. Geburtstag am 17. November 1967*, 200–206. Hrsg. von Gerhard Müller und Winfried Zeller. Leiden: Brill, 1967.

C27   "The Responsibilities of Power According to Erasmus of Rotterdam." In *The Responsibility of Power; Historical Essays in Honor of Hajo Holborn*, 54–63. Edited by Leonard Krieger and Fritz Stern. Garden City, N.Y.: Double-day, 1967.

1968

C28   "The Complexity of the Reformation." In *The Reformation: Revival or Rev-olution?*, 37–45. Edited by W. Stanford Reid. New York: Rinehart and Winston, 1968. European Problem Studies.

1969

C29   "Correspondence...." In *In Remembrance of Reu; An Evaluation of the Life and Work of J. Michael Reu, 1869-1943, on the 100th Anniversary of His Birth by Some of His Friends and Former Students*, 25. Edited by Robert C. Wiederaenders. Dubuque, Ia.: Wartburg Seminary Association, 1969.

C30   "The De-Formation of Christianity." In *Toward a Working Theology: The John Hadden Leith Lecture Series*, 1–6. Auburn, Ala.: First Presbyterian Church, 1969.

C31   "Erasmus and the Persecuted." In *Scrinium Erasmianum; Mélanges his-toriques publiés sous la patronage de l'Université de Louvain*, 2:197–202. Edited by J. Coppens. Leiden: Brill, 1969.

C32   "The Problem of Authority in the Age of the Reformation." In *Luther, Erasmus and the Reformation: A Catholic-Protestant Reappraisal*, 14–25. Edited by John C. Olin, James D. Smart, and Robert E. McNally. New York: Fordham University Press, 1969.

C33   "Wilbrandis Rosenblatt." In *Gottesreich und Menschenreich; Ernst Staehelin zum 80. Geburtstag*, 71–86. Hrsg. von Max Geiger. Basel: Verlag Helbing and Lichtenhahn, 1969.

1970

C34   "Katherine Zell." In *In Honor of S. Harrison Thomson,* 3–28. Edited by Paul Maurice Clogan. Cleveland: Press of Case Western Reserve University, 1970. Medievalia et Humanistica, n.s., no. 1.

C35   "Men and Cities of the Reformation." In *The Renaissance: Maker of Modern Man,* 287–96. Washington: National Geographic Society,1970.

1971

C36   "Die frühe Kirche und der Krieg." In *Das frühe Christentum in römischen Staat,* 187–216. Compiled by Richard Klein. Darmstadt: Wissenschaftliches Buchges., 1971. Wege der Forschung, Bd. 267.

    — Original English edition entitled "The Early Church and War." *Harvard Theological Review* 39 (July 1946): 189–212.

    — Also published in *The Church, the Gospel, and War.* See C6.

    — Reprinted. New York: Garland, 1971. The Garland Library of War and Peace.

1972

C37   "John Foxe and the Ladies." In *Social History of the Reformation* [in honor of Harold J. Grimm], 208–22. Edited by Lawrence P. Buch and Jonathan W. Zophy. Columbus: Ohio State University Press, 1972.

C38   "Neuere Lutherbiographien und Darstellungen der Geschichte der Reformation." In *Luthers Stellung zu den Juden im Spiegel seiner Interpreten: Interpretation und Rezeption von Luthers Schriften und Ausserungen zum Judentum im 19. und 20. Jahrhundert vor allem im deutschsprachigen Raum,* 311–12. München: M. Hueber, 1972.

1973

C39   "Queen Katerina Jagellonica (Sweden), 1526-1583." In *Theological Soundings; Notre Dame Seminary Jubilee Studies, 1923–1973,* 48–62. Presented by the Faculty of the School of Theology. Edited by June Mihalik. New Orleans: Notre Dame Seminary, 1973.

    — This article was delivered as two papers in 1973 in the Notre Dame Distinguished Lecture Series.

1975

C40   "Feminine Piety in Tudor England." In *Christian Spirituality: Essays in Honor of Gordon Rupp*, 183–201. Edited by Peter Brooks. London SCM, 1975.

C41   "Jonathan Edwards: 'The Great Awakening.'" in *Essays in American Intellectual History*, 58–65. Edited by Wilson Smith. Hinsdale, Ill.: Dryden Press, 1975.

1976

C42   "Piety and Art." In *Traditio-Krisis-Renovatio aus theologischer Sicht: Festschrift Winfried Zeller zum 65. Geburtstag*, 609–12. Hrsg. Bernd Jaspert und Rudolf Mohr. Marburg: N.G. Elwert, 1976.

1977

C43   "Psychiatry and History: An Examination of Erikson's Young Man Luther." In *Psychohistory and Religion: The Case of Young Man Luther*, 19–56. Edited by Roger A. Johnson. Philadelphia: Fortress, 1977.

— Photocopy. Ann Arbor, Mich.: University Microfilms International, 1988.

1979

C44   "A Letter from Roland Bainton—on Immortality." In *Continuity and Discontinuity in Church History*, 390–96. Presented to George Huntston Williams. Leiden: Brill, 1979.

— This article surveys the first fifty years of the Ingersoll lectures on immortality.

1980

C44.4   "Learned Women in the Europe of the Sixteenth Century." In *Beyond Their Sex: Learned Women of the European Past*, 117–28. Edited by Patricia H. Labalme. New York: New York University Press, 1980.

C44.5   "The Left Wing of the Reformation." In *The Anabaptists and Thomas Müntzer*, 41–45. Translated and edited by James M. Stayer and Werner O. Packull. Dubuque, Ia. and Toronto: Kendall/Hunt, 1980.

C44.6   "Luther: Pastor, Consoler, Preacher." In *Encounters with Luther, 1: Lectures, Discussions and Sermons,* 173–80, Martin Luther Colloquia, 1970–74. Edited by Eric W. Gritsch. Gettysburg, Pa.: Institute for Luther Studies, 1980.

ON TEACHING AND WRITING

1946

C44.9   "'Poppy Burr': George Lincoln Burr." In *Great Teachers, portrayed by those who studied under them,* 173–83. Edited with an introduction by Houston Peterson. New Brunswick, N.J.: Rutgers University Press, 1946.

1955

C45   "The School of Divinity." In *Seventy-Five: A Study of a Generation in Transition,* 25–26, 166–68. New Haven: *Yale Daily News,* 1955.

1956

C46   "Religious Biography." In *Writing for the Religious Market,* 185–89. Edited by Roland E. Wolseley. New York: Association Press, 1956.

1961

C47   "Luther and Education." In *New Dimensions in Lutheran Higher Education, 1910–1965,* 11–18. Papers presented at the Golden Anniversary Convention of the National Lutheran Education Conference, 10–12 January 1960. Washington: National Lutheran Educational Conference, 1961.

1975

C48   "A Word from Roland Bainton." In *Yale Divinity School: Leadership in American Religion, The Great Yale Tradition,* 26. New Haven: Campaign for Yale, 1975.

ISSUES OF WAR AND PEACE

1948

C49   "The Early Church and War." In *The Church, the Gospel and War,* 79–92. Edited by Rufus M. Jones. New York: Harper, 1948.

1953

C50   "War and the Christian Ethic." In *The Church and Social Responsibility,* 79–92. Edited by Rufus M. Jones. New York: Harper, 1948.

— For further information see C6.

1961

C51   "From Outlawry of War to A-Bomb." In *God and the H-Bomb*, 24–34. Edited by Donald Keys. Published by Bellmeadows Press with Bernard Gels Associates. Distributed by Ransom House, 1961.

C52   "The Ultimate Folly." In *Therefore Choose Life: Essays on the Nuclear Crisis*, 5–7. By Roland H. Bainton and others. London: International Fellowship of Reconciliation, 1961.

1966

C53   "Truth, Freedom, and Tolerance: The View of a Protestant." In *War, Poverty, Freedom: The Christian Response*, 17–29. New York: Paulist Press, 1966. Concilium; Theology in the Age of Renewal: Moral Theology, vol. 15.

CONCERNS OF THE PASTORAL MINISTRY

1945

C54   "The Churches and Alcohol." In *Alcohol, Science, and Society*, Twenty-Nine Lectures with Discussions as Given at the Yale Summer School of Alcohol Studies, 287–98. New Haven: Quarterly Journal of Studies on Alcohol, 1945.

— Published also in *Quarterly Journal of Studies on Alcohol* 6 (June 1945): 45–58. See D104.

— Published later in *Social Progress* 39 (November 1948): 13–19. See 105.5.

— Reprinted in *Collected Papers III*, 165–86, combined with another article after reworking. See A29.

1953

C55   "Christianity and Sex: An Historical Survey." In *Sex and Religion Today*, 17–96. Edited by Simon Doniger. New York: Association Press, 1953. Pastoral Psychology Series.

     — First published as an article in *Pastoral Psychology* 3 (September 1952): 10–26; and 4 (February 1953): 12–29. See D106.

Undated

C56   "The Ministry of Mr. Bainton." In *First Congregational Church, Cheshire, Ct. 250th Anniversary, 1724–1974*, 22–28. (n.p.: n.d.).

     — This article concerns Herbert Bainton, the author's father.

POPULAR FAITH AND PREACHING

1959

C57   "Luther and Ourselves." In *Best Sermons, Volume VII, 1959–1960*, 222–28. Protestant Edition. Edited by G. Paul Butler. New York: Thomas Y. Crowell, 1959.

1963

C58   [Scattered Selections] in *Images of Faith: Illustrations of the Christian Faith by Contemporary Christian Thinkers*, 21–22, 79–83, 114–15, 224–25. Compiled and edited by Wendell Mathews and Robert P. Wetzler. St. Louis: Concordia Publishing House, 1963.

C59   [Statement] in *Bible Words that Guide Me*, 11–12. Edited by Hubert A. Elliot. New York: Grosset and Dunlap, 1963.

1964

C60   "Pictures of Jesus." In *Best Sermons, Volume IX, 1964*, 159–65. Protestant Edition. Edited by G. Paul Butler. Princeton, Van Nostrand, 1964.

1968

C61   "Thanksgiving." In *Best Sermons, Volume X, 1966–1968*, 370–74. Protestant Edition. Edited by G. Paul Butler. New York: Trident Press, 1968.

THE CHURCH AND SOCIETY

1958

C62   "The Making of a Pluralistic Society—A Protestant View." In *Religion and the State University*, 42–47. Edited by Erich Albert Walter. Ann Arbor: University of Michigan Press, 1958.

—   Reprinted in *Collected Papers III*, 100–105. See A29.

Photo Yale Divinity School. Used by permission.

D. ARTICLES PUBLISHED IN PERIODICALS

STUDIES IN CHURCH HISTORY

1923

D1   "Basilidian Chronology and New Testament Interpretation." *Journal of Biblical Literature* 42 (1923): 81–134. See also A1.

1925

D2   "What is Calvinism?" *Christian Century* 42 (12 March 12 1925): 351–52.

— Letter to the editor in response to an article of 14 February entitled "What is Calvinism?"

1929

D3   "The Development and Consistency of Luther's Attitudes to Religious Liberty." *Harvard Theological Review* 22 (April 1929): 107–49.

— Reprinted in *Collected Papers II*, 20–45, under the title "Luther's Attitudes on Religious Liberty." See A28.

— A response to this article is found in *Revue d'histoire ecclésiastique* 26 (January 1930): 219–20, written by A. Faux.

1930

D4   "The Immoralities of the Patriarchs according to the Exegesis of the late Middle Ages and the Reformation." *Harvard Theological Review* 23 (January 1930): 39–49.

— Reprinted in *Collected Papers I*, 122–33, under the title "Interpretations of the Immoralities of the Patriarchs." See A26.

1931

D5   "The Smaller Circulation: Servetus and Colombo." *Sudhoffs Archiv für Geschichte der Medezin* 24 (1931): 371–74.

D6   "William Postell and the Netherlands." *Nederlandsch Archief voor Kerkgeschiedenis* 29 (1931): 161–72.

— Reprinted in *Collected Papers II*, 185–98. See A28.

1932

D7   "The Parable of the Tares as the Proof Text for Religious Liberty to the End of the Sixteenth Century." *Church History* 1 (June 1932): 67–89.

— Reprinted in *Collected Papers I*, 95–121, under the title "Religious Liberty and the Parable of the Tares." See A26.

D8   "The Present State of Servetus Studies." *Journal of Modern History* 4 (March 1932): 72–92.

— Reviewed by M. Bataillon in *Bulletin Hispanique* 34 (1932): 329–31.

1936

D9   "Changing Ideas and Ideals in the Sixteenth Century." *Journal of Modern History* 8 (December 1936): 417–43.

— Reprinted in *Collected Papers I*, 159–82.

D10   "Servetus and the Genevan Libertines." *Church History* 5 (June 1936): 141–49.

— French translation published in *Bulletin de la Société de l'Histoire du Protestantisme Français* 87 (July/September 1938): 261–69.

1938

D11   "New Documents on Early Protestant Rationalism." *Church History* 7 (June 1938): 179–87.

— Reprinted in *Collected Papers II* with one paragraph omitted, 130–38. See A28.

D12   "Unity, Utrecht and the Unitarians." *Christian Century* 55 (5 October 1938): 1189–90.

— Reprinted in *Collected Papers III*, 51–56. See A29.

1939

D13   "Reformationshistorische Studien in den Vereinigten Staaten." *Archiv für Reformationsgeschichte* 36 (1939): 280–82.

1940

D14   "Congregationalism: The Middle Way." *Christendom* 5 (summer 1940): 345–54.

1941

D15   "Classical and Biblical Scholarship in the Age of the Renaissance and Reformation." *Church History*, 10 (1941): 125–43.

    — Written jointly with Dean P. Lockwood.

    — Reprinted in *Collected Papers I* with two paragraphs omitted under the title "Biblical Scholarship in the Renaissance and Reformation," 210–16. See A28.

D16   "The Left Wing of the Reformation." *Journal of Religion* 21 (April 1941): 124–234.

    — Reprinted in *Collected Papers III*, 119–29. See A29.

    — Reprinted again in *The Anabaptists and Thomas Müntzer.* Edited by James M. Stayer and Werner O. Packull. See C44.5.

D17   "The Struggle for Religious Liberty." *Church History* 10 (June 1941): 95–124.

    — Reprinted in *Collected Papers II*, 211–42. See A28.

1941–42

D18   "Christian Views of Human Destiny." *Religion in Life* 11 (Winter 1941–42): 96–105.

    — Reprinted in *Collected Papers I*, 83–94.

1943

D19   "Bossuet and Leibniz and the Reunion of the Churches." *The Chronicle* (Protestant Episcopal), 43 (February 1943): 102–104.

    — Reprinted in *Collected Papers III*, 43–48. See A29.

D20   "Congregationalism: From the Just War to the Crusade in the Puritan Revolution." *Andover-Newton Theological School Bulletin* 35 (April 1943): 1–20.

— Delivered as part of the Southworth Lectures.

— Reprinted in *Collected Papers II*, 248–74, under the title "Congregationalism and the Puritan Revolution from the Just War to the Crusade." See A28.

1946

D21   "Early Christianity as a Youth Movement." *Highroad* (February 1946): 35–37.

D22   "The Early Church and War." *Harvard Theological Review* 39 (July 1946): 189–212.

— For further information see C6.

D23   "Eyn wunderliche Weyssagung Osiander-Sachs-Luther." *Germanic Review* 21 (October 1946): 161–64.

— Reprinted in English in *Collected Papers II*, 62–66, under the title "The Joachimite Prophecy: Osiander and Sachs." See A28.

D24   "The Sectarian Theory of the Church." *Christendom* 11 (summer 1946): 382–87.

1947

D25   "Dürer and Luther as the Man of Sorrows." *Art Bulletin* 29 (December 1947): 269–72.

— Reprinted in *Collected Papers II*, 51–61 under the title "The Man of Sorrows in Dürer and Luther." See A28.

D26   "Let's Agree on the Reformation!" *Christian Century* 64 (19 February 1947): 237–39.

D28   "Luther's Struggle for Faith." *Church History* 17 (September 1948): 193–206.

— For further information see C8.

1949

D29   "Luther and the *Via Media* at the Marburg Colloquy." *Lutheran Quarterly* 1 (November 1949): 394–98.

— Reprinted in *Collected Papers II*, 46–50. See A28.

D30   "Martin Luther: The Appropriateness of His Christmas Sermons in 1949." *American-German Review* 16 (December 1949): 3–4.

D31   "The Puritan Theocracy and the Cambridge Platform." *The Minister's Quarterly* 5 (February 1949): 16–21.

— For further information see C7.

1950

D32   "Here I Stand." *Newsweek* 36 (13 November 1950): 2 and 6.

— Letter to the editor refuting statements published concerning *Here I Stand.*

1951

D33   "Ernst Troeltsch—Thirty Years Later." *Theology Today* 8 (April 1951): 70–96.

— Reprinted in *Collected Papers III*, 125–53, under the title "Ernst Troeltsch—Thirty Years Later: A Critique of the Social Teaching of the Christian Churches." See A29.

D34   "Josiah Willard Gibbs." *Yale Divinity News* 46 (March 1951): 4–5.

D35   "Michael Servetus and the Pulmonary Transit of the Blood." *Bulletin of the History of Medicine* 25 (January/February 1951): 1–7.

— Read as the Fielding H. Garrison Lecture at the twenty-third annual meeting of the American Association of the History of Medecine, Boston, 22 May 1950.

D36   "The *Querela Pacis* of Erasmus, Classical and Christian Sources." *Archiv für Reformationsgeschichte* 42 (1951): 32–49.

— Reprinted in *Collected Papers I*, 217–35, under the title "The Complaint of Peace of Erasmus, Classical and Christian Sources." See A26.

D37   "Recent Books in Church History." *Yale Divinity News* 46 (January 1951): 6.

1952

D38   "Luther in a Capsule." *Bulletin of the American Congregational Association* 3 (May 1952): 3–9.

D39   "Der Mass des Mannes Gottes." *Pastoral Theology* 41 (January 1952): 1–3.

D40   "The Reformation and Politics." *Pulpit Digest* 32 (May 1952): 11–16.

— This article is a chapter taken from *The Reformation of the Sixteenth Century*. See A13.

D41   "Sebastian Castellio and the British-American Tradition." *Het Boek* 30 (1952): 347–49.

D42   "Survey of Periodical Literature in the United States, 1945–1951." *Archiv für Reformationsgeschichte* 43 (1952): 88–106.

1953

D43   "Anabaptist Source Materials." *Mennonite Life* 8 (July 1953): inside back cover.

D44   "Burned Heretic: Michael Servetus." *Christian Century* 70 (28 October 1953): 1230–31.

D45   "The Church of the Restoration." *Mennonite Life* 8 (July 1953): 136–43.

— Delivered as part of the Menno Simons Lecture Series at Bethel College, North Newton, Kansas in 1952. It has been published here in a series of articles entitled "The Beginnings of Anabaptism."

D46   "L'Esprit d'un Congrès." *Le Protestante* (Geneva) (15 August 1953): 1.

D47   "The Great Commission." *Mennonite Life* 8 (October 1953): 183–89.

— Includes photograph of RHB at a dinner given in his honor during the Menno Simons Lectures, 183.

— For further information see D45.

D48   "To the Editor." *American Historical Review* 58 (July 1953): 1055–56.

— Response to G. D. Sellery's review of *The Reformation of the Sixteenth Century*. See P25.

1953–54

D49   "Documenta Servetiana." *Archiv für Reformationsgeschichte* 44 (1953): 223–34, pt. 1; and 45 (1954): 99–108 pt. 2.

1954

D50   "Catholic-Protestant Relations in the United States," a syndicated article appearing in several journals including the following: *Advance* 146 (18 October 1954): 13–24; *Lutheran Tidings* (20 October 1954); *The Walther League Messenger* 19 (October 1954): 14–17.

D51   "The Enduring Witness: The Mennonites." *Mennonite Life* 9 (April 1954): 83–90.

— For further information see D46.

D52   "The Frontier Community." *Mennonite Life* 9 (January 1954): 34–41.

— For further information see D46.

D53   "Is Congregatonalism Sectarian?" *Christian Century* 71 (24 February 1954): 234–48.

D54   "Man, God and the Church in the Age of the Renaissance." *Journal of Religious Thought* 11 (spring/summer 1954): 119–33.

— For further information see C10.

1955

D55   "Freedom, Truth, and Unity: Reflections on the Renaissance." *Theology Today* 12 (April 1955): 85–96.

— Reprinted in *Collected Papers I*, 230–48. See A26.

1956

D56   "Critical Comments on Dr. R. Hooykaas' 'Science and Reformation.'" *Journal of World History* 3 (1956): 109–41.

D57   "The Office of the Minister's Wife in New England." *Harvard Divinity School Bulletin* 21 (5 November 1956): 37–59.

— Delivered as the Dudleian Lecture, 1954–55.

— Reprinted in *Collected Papers III*, 265–82. See A29.

1957

D58   "Alexander Campbell and Church Unity." *Ecumenical Studies Series* 3 (January 1957): 19–29. See also C17.

D59   "The Universal Ministry of All Believers." *Encounter* 18 (spring 1957): 131–40.

1958

D60   "Thomas Hooker and the Puritan Contribution to Democracy." *Bulletin of the Congregational Library* 10 (October 1958): 5–15.

— Reprinted in *Collected Papers III*, 239–51.

1960

D61   "Interpretations of the Reformation." *American Historical Review* 66 (October 1960): 74–84.

— Reprinted 1960. Indianapolis: Bobbs-Merrill Reprint Series on European History: Reformation, no. 1.

— Reprinted in *Collected Papers II*, 104–16.

— Portuguese translation by Sylvio Pedrozo. Under the title "Diferentes Interpretações da Reforma." *Revista Teológica Campinas* (Brazil) 22 (December 1960): 97–109.

— For further information see C21.

1961

D62   "Mission in Latin America." *Christian Century* 78:2.

— (11 January 1961): 41–4 (pt. 1) and 78:3

— (18 January 1961): 78–80 (pt. 2).

D63   "Statement." *Bulletin*. Department of Theology, World Presbyterian Alliance and the World Alliance of Reformed Churches 2 (summer 1961): 12.

1962

D63.5 "Harold S. Bender, 1897–1962" [obituary]. *Church History* 31 (December 1962): 476.

D64   "Luther and Spalatin Letters Recovered in Boston." Communicated by RHB. *Archiv fur Reformationsgeschichte* 53 (1967): 197.

D65   "The Meaning of the Life and Work of Harold S. Bender: A Symposium," by RHB et al. *Mennonite Quarterly Review* 38 (1964): 175 (RHB's statement).

1966

D66   "The Paraphrases of Erasmus." Archiv für Reformationsgeschichte 57 (1966): 67–75.

1967

D67   "Erasmo e l'Italia." Translated by Daniele Pianciola. *Rivista Storica Italiana* 79 (1967): 944–51.

1968

D68   "Continuity of Thought in Erasmus." *ACLS Newsletter* (American Council of Learned Societies) 19 (May 1968): 1–7.

1969

D68.5   "Kenneth Scott Latourette" [obituary]. *Church History* 38 (March 1969).

1971

D69   "Psychiatry and History: An Examination of Erikson's Young Man Luther." *Religion and Life* 40 (winter 1971): 450–78.

D70   "Vittoria Colonna and Michelangelo." *Forum* (A Special Renaissance Issue) 9 (spring 1971): 34–41.

   — Taken from *Women of the Reformation in Germany and Italy* and printed in advance with permission of the publisher. See A32.

1972

D71   "The Role of Women in the Reformation: Introduction to the Following Three Papers." *Archiv für Reformationsgeschichte* 63 (1972): 141–42.

1973

D72   "Luther und seine Mutter." Berechtige übersetzung aus dem Amerikanischen von Elisabeth Langerbeck. *Luther,* Heft 3 (1973): 123–30.

D73   "Luther und sein Vater: Psychiatrie und Biographie." Übersetzung aus dem
Amerikanischen von Elisabeth Langerbeck. *Zeitwende* 44 (November
1973): 393– 403.

1981–83

D73.5 "Luther, Begin and the Jews." *Christianity and Crisis* 41 (5 October 1981):
270–71.

— "The Prime Minister and the Professor—Luther and the Jews: An
Exchange" [Begin's reply]. *Christianity and Crisis* 42 (15 March 1982):
70.

— This exchange of letters was reprinted in *Lutheran Theological
Review* (spring 1983).

— Reprinted from above in *Lutheran Theological Journal* 17 (December 1983): 131–39.

D73.6 "Rediscovering our Roots in Search of a Future" [discussion]. *Japan Christian Quarterly* 47 (fall 1981).

— This issue edited by David L. Swain and entitled "The Church in
Japan and Asia's Future." Fellowship of Christian Missionaries in
Japan. Conference, 29–31 July.

D73.7 "Thomas Müntzer: Revolutionary Firebrand of the Reformation." *Sixteenth Century Journal* 13 (summer 1982): 3–15.

On Teaching and Writing

1932

D74   "Methods of Great Religious Teachers." *International Journal of Religious
Education* 9 (September 1932): 6–7 (Luther); (November 1932): 6–7
(Calvin); and (December 1932): 19–20 (Loyola).

1935

D75   "Academic Freedom in the Light of the Struggle for Religious Liberty." *Proceedings of the Middle States Association of History Teachers* 33 (1935): 37–44.

1941

D76   "Man and World Remaking: Evening Lectures by Dr. Roland Bainton." *The Hazen Conferences on Student Guidance and Counseling* (1941): 44–55.

1942

D77   "Teaching Church History." *Journal of Bible and Religion* 10 (May 1942): 103–107.

1959

D78   "Teaching Seminarians Public Speech." *Yale Divinity News* (March 1959): 7.

— Includes pen and ink sketches as well as text.

1960

D79   "Working with the Eternal Word." *Saturday Review* 43 (5 March 1960): 27.

1962

D79.5 "Dedication Address of New Library at University of Vermont." *University of Vermont Alumni Magazine* (January 1962): 10–12, 17.

ISSUES OF WAR AND PEACE

1938

D80   "Refugees of Other Days." *Bulletin of the Story Behind the Headlines* 2 (13 December 1938): 14–20.

— Whole issue is called "Appeasement Comes to France."

D81   "Technology and Pacifism." *Christian Century* 55 (18 May 1938): 618–19.

1942

D82   "A Communication for a More Explicit Declaration of Peace Aims." *Christian Century* 59 (16 September 1942): 1122–24.

— The argument of this statement, which was issued after the bombing of Pearl Harbor, is summarized by RHB in his autobiography, *Roly* (see A39). Other prominent faculty at Yale Divinity School were among the signers.

1943

D83   "The Churches Shift on War." *Religion in Life* 12 (summer 1943): 1–13.

— Reprinted in *Collected Papers III*, 187–200. See A29.

D84   "Reconciliation and Reality." *Fellowship* 9 (December 1943): 208–10.

1944

D85   "The Christian and War." *Christian Century* 61 (3 May 1944): 559–61.

D86   "The Relation of the Church to the War in Light of the Christian Faith." *Social Action* 10 (15 December 1944): 5–79.

1945

D87   "The Churches and War: Historic Attitudes toward Christian Participation, A Survey from Biblical Times to the Present Day." *Social Action* 9 (15 January 1945): 5–71.

— Also printed separately under the same title. New York, 1945. 71 pages.

1946

D88   "The Early Church and War." *Harvard Theological Review* 39 (July 1946): 189–212.

— For further information see C6.

1949

D89   "Christmas in 1949." *The American German Review* 16 (December 1949): 3–4.

— Postwar reflections.

D90   "Without Despairing of the World: The Quaker Attitude toward Peace and War." *Friends Intelligencer* 106 (12 2d mo. 1949): 87–89.

— A similar article appeared in German entitled "Die Stellung der Quaker zu Krieg und Frieden." *Der Quaker* 23 (January/February 1949): 1–7.

1958

D91   "Christian Pacifism Reassessed." *Christian Century* 75 (23 July 1958): 847–49.

D92   "Early Church Was Pacifist." *Christian Century* 75 (10 September 1958): 1029.

— This article is a defense of RHB's earlier article (see above, D91) in response to critique.

D93   "Neue Erwägungen zum Thema 'Christlicher Pazifismus.'" *Junge Kirche* 19 (10 November 1958): 564–70.

D94   "Reafirmaçao de Pacifismo Cristao." *Unitas* 20 (1958): 26–34.

1960

D95   "From Outlawry of War to A-Bomb." *Christian Century* 77 (28 September 1960): 1112–15.

— Excerpted from *Christian Attitudes toward War and Peace*. See A22.

1962

D96   "The Will to Peace." *Fellowship* 26 (1 November 1960): 13–16 and 34.

D97   "McCrackin before the Assembly." *Christian Century* 79 (18 April 1962): 488–90.

— Concerns activity in the United Presbyterian Church.

1963

D98   "Statement on the Revocation by the Internal Revenue Service of the Fellowship of Reconciliation's Status as a Tax-Exempt Organization," *Continuum* 1 (Autumn 1963).

— RHB joined others in issuing this statement.

1966

D99   "Is the War in Vietnam Just? A Reply to Mr. Little by Roland H. Bainton."
       The Limb (Yale Divinity School) 2 (Autumn 1966): 1–3.

D100   "Viet Aid—Pro and Con." *New Haven Register* (25 October 1966): 14.

       — Letter to the editor.

1969

D100.7 "Townsman Coffin." *New Haven Register* (16 January 1969).

       — Letter to the editor.

1971

D101   "Bishop A. F. Winnington-Ingram." *Theology* 74 (January 1971): 32–33.

       — Reply by D. Y. Thompson (June 1974): 264–65.

1972

D102   "Reassessing 'Pacifism Reassessed.'" *Christian Century* 89 (17 May 1972):
       575–77.

1973

D102.1 "Letter to the Editor." *New York Times* (3 June 1973): sec. 4, p. 16.

       — Signed jointly with Harry Rudin.

1981

D102.2 "Taking a Risk for Peace." *Center Magazine* 14 (March/April 1981): 2–4.

1982

D102.3 "Biblical/Theological Analysis of Implications of Militarized Society:
       Christian Attitudes toward National Defense." *Engage/Social Action* (April
       1982). See D102.5.

D102.5 "A Juggling Match to See Who Can Unbalance the Balance: A Biblical
       Scholar Views the 'Balance of Power'(excerpt), in 'The Mad Arms Race:
       Formula for Destruction'" (Engage/Social Action Forum 81). *Engage/Social
       Action* 10 (April 1982): 9–40.

CONCERNS OF THE PASTORAL MINISTRY

1918

D103   "The Ministry of Thought." *Yale Divinity Quarterly* 15 (May 1918): 1–5.

1945

D104   "The Churches and Alcohol." *Quarterly Journal of Studies on Alcohol* 6 (June 1945): 45–58.

— For further information see C54.

1948

D105   "Marriage and Love in Christian History." *Religion in Life* 17 (summer 1948): 391–403.

1952–53

D106   "Christianity and Sex: An Historical Survey." *Pastoral Psychology* 3 (September 1952): 10–26; 4 (February 1953): 12–19.

— For further information, see C55.

D107   "The Minister and Alcoholic Beverages." *The Union Signal* 79 (22 April 1953): 30.

— A chapel talk first published in *The Connecticut Citizen.*

— Also in *The Voice* 42 (December 1954): 8–9.

1955

D108   "Pappi ja Vakijuomat." *Raitis Ylioppilas* (Helsinki) (1955): 2–3 (unnumbered).

— Concerns alcohol.

1958

D109   "Sex and Religion: Three Christian Views of Love, Sex and Marriage." *Ladies Home Journal* 75 (August 1958): 17, 100–101.

D110   "Total Abstinence and Biblical Principles." *Christianity Today* 2 (7 July 1958): 3–6.

— Reprinted in *Collected Papers III*, 165–86. See A29.

POPULAR FAITH AND PREACHING

1938

D111   "Straightforward Speech." *Yale Divinity News* 34 (May 1938): 1–3.

— Notes from a series of chapel talks.

1945

D112   "The Cohesive Power of Protestantism." *The Intercollegian* 62 (January 1945): 8–9.

1946

D113   "Our Debt to Luther." *Christian Century* 63 (23 October 1946): 1276–78.

1948

D114   "Our Protestant Witness." *The Pulpit* 19 (December 1948): 272–74.

1950

D115   "The Genius of Protestantism." *Minister's Quarterly* 6 (February 1950): 13–18.

1951

D116   "Christian Adversatives." *Oberlin Alumni Bulletin* 9 (1951): 2–3.

1953

D117   "A Book, Bitter and Sweet." *Fellowship* (September 1953): 20–22.

D118   "Protestant List for Lent: Roland H. Bainton Selects 26 Titles." *Christian Advocate* 312 (5 March 1953: 24.

D119   "Protestant Reading List." *Saturday Review* (21 February 1953): 50.

1959

D120   "Are Moral Laws Immortal?" *True Story* (November 1959): 41.

D121   "Mistrust of Catholicism." *Christian Register* (Unitarian) (October 1959): 16–18.

1960

D122   "On the Celebration of Christmas: From Martin Luther." *Christian Century* 77 (21 December 1960: 1491–92.

— One of several contributions written in the form of letters from historical figures.

1962

D123   "Don't Tell Me the Old, Old Story, Sing Me a New Song." *Faith at Work* (March 1962): 30–32.

D123.5 "Renewal of Faith." *How* (March 1962): 1–2.

— Reprinted from *Yale Divinity News* (March 1961).

1968

D124   "Thank and Think." *Holden Village Courier* (Advent 1968): 8–12.

— Devotional talks.

1973–74

D125   "The Incarnation." *Cross Talk* 2 (December/January/February 1973–74): n.p.

D125.4 "Resurrection on Canvas." *Hartford Courant Sunday* (14 April 1974).

1978

D125.5 "The Meaning of Resurrection." *Cross Talk* 7 (March–May 1978).

THE CHURCH AND SOCIETY

1940

D126   "Christian Conscience and the State." *Social Action* (15 October 1940): 4–42.

1942

D127   "Individualism, Christian and American." *Vital Speeches of the Day* 8 (15 July 1942): 590–92.

1943

D128   "The Four Freedoms." *Girls Today* 2 (July 1943) (pt. 1); 2 (August 1943) (pt. 2); 2 (September 1943) (pt. 3); and 2 (October 1943) (pt. 4).

1949

D129   "Christianity and Russian Communism." *Journal of the Industrial and Social Order Council of the Society of Friends* 6 (March/April 1949): 6–11.

1954

D130   "Letter to the Editor." *Advance* 146 (5 April 1954): 26.

— Concerns the role of social action in Congregationalism and addresses questions raised by the League to Uphold Congregational Principles.

1955

D131   "The Religious Foundations of Freedom." *Christian Century* 72 (26 January 1955): 106–109.

1959

D132   "Religion and the State University," comments by RHB and others. *Information Service* (National Council of Churches) (14 February 1959): 7.

1960

D133   "Basic Issues in the Uphaus Case." *New Haven Register* (24 January 1960): 18.

1966

D134   "Truth, Freedom and Tolerance: The View of a Protestant." *Concilium* 5 (May 1966): 11–17.

CONCERNING QUAKERS

1947

D135   "What Does a Quaker Believe?" *New Haven Register* (11 May 1947): 2, 9.

1949

D136   "Without Despairing of the World: Quaker Attitude toward Peace and War." *Friends Intelligencer* 106 (12 2d mo. 1949): 87–89.

— For further information see D90.

1958

D137   "Friends in Relation to the Churches." *Inward Light* 21 (spring 1958): 29–40.

— For further information see A16.

1966

D138   "The Future of Quakerism." *Quaker Religious Thought* 8 (Autumn 1966): 2–9.

1974

D139   "Integrity of Membership." *Christian Century* 91 (13 February 1974): 187.

— Letter to the editor and reply to Richard Nixon and the Quaker Fellowship.

CONCERNING YALE

1955

D140   "The Grand Errand." *Yale Alumni Magazine* (October 1955): 22–23.

1956

D141   "Yale and German Theology in the Middle of the Nineteenth Century." *Zeitschrift für Kirchengeschichte* 65 (1956): 294–302.

— Reprinted in *Collected Papers III*, 252–64. See A29.

1959

D142 　"Halford Luccock." *Yale Divinity News* (November 1959): 106–109.

　　　— Includes sketch of Luccock (see figure at *left*).

Halford Luccock
by RHB

D143 　"Our Helpers of Yester Years." *Yale Divinity News* (January 1959): 10.

D144 　"Timothy Dwight the Younger." *Yale Divinity News* (May 1959): 20.

　　　— Includes sketch.

1960

D145 　"Clarence Shedd." *Yale Divinity News* (March 1960): 7.

1965

D146 　"Tribute to Robert Calhoun." *Yale Divinity News* (May 1965): 3–4.

　　　— Includes sketch of Calhoun.

1966

D146.5 "George Pierson 1883–1966." *Reflection* (November 1966): 11.

Robert Calhoun,
by RHB

1971

D147 　"The Yale Strike." *Commonweal* 95 (5 November 1971): 123, 142–43.

　　　— Letter to the editor responding to Dennis Hale's critique of Yale's behavior in the strike.

1977

D147.5 [Statement by RHB; caption to his photograph portrait], in "Professors Emeriti." Photography by Phyllis Crowley, *Yale Alumni Magazine* (October 1977): 14. See also O29.5.

MISCELLANEOUS

1941

D147.7   "David Schley Schaaf" [obituary]. *The American Historical Review* (July 1941).

1944

D148   "Easter: In Many Climes and Times." *Girls Today* 3 (9 April 1944): 1, 6.

1945

D149   "The Amistad." *Highroad* (September 1945): 4–6, 47.

1968

D150   "Rhymes and Ripples of Japan." *Japan Christian Quarterly* 34 (spring 1968): 104–11.

1975

D151   "What Dr. Bainton Saw" and "Polish Rebuilding National Soul." *New Haven Register* (25 May 1975): sec. A. P10.

1978

D152   "Christmas Art in Asia." *New Haven Register* (24 December 1978): E8.

E. ARTICLES PUBLISHED IN ENCYCLOPEDIAS
AND DICTONARIES

1934

E1   "Mitchell, Jonathan." In *Dictionary of American Biography*, edited by Dumas Malone, 19:55–56. New York: Scribner's, 1934.

E2   "Mombert, Jacob Isador." In *Dictionary of American Biography*, edited by Dumas Malone, 13:82–83. New York: Scribner's, 1934.

E3   "Murdock, James." In *Dictionary of American Biography*, edited by Dumas Malone, 13:342. New York: Scribner's, 1934.

E4   "Walker, Williston." In *Dictionary of American Biography*, edited by Dumas Malone, 19:366–67. New York: Scribner's, 1934.

1955–59

E5   "Augsburg." In *The Mennonite Encyclopedia: A Comprehensiv Reference Work on the Anabaptist-Mennonite Movement*, 1:185. Hillsboro, Ks.: Mennonite Brethren Publication Office, 1955–59.

E6   "Marpeck Pilgrim." In *The Mennonite Encyclopedia: A Comprehensive Reference Work on the Anabaptist-Mennonite Movement*, 3:492. Hillsboro, Ks.: Mennonite Brethren Publication Office, 1955–59.

E6.5 "Servetus, Michael (1511–53)." In *The Mennonite Encyclopedia: A Comprehensive Reference Work on the Anabaptist-Mennonite Movement*, 4:506–507. Scottsdale, Pa.: Mennonite Publishing House, 1959.

1961

E7   "Renaissance und Religion." In *Die Religion in Geschichte und Gegenwart: Handwörterbuch für Theologie und Religionswissenschaft*, 1061–63. 3. Aufl. Tübingen: Mohr Sieback, 1957–, Band V, 1961.

— Reprinted in *Collected Papers I*, 204–209, under the title "The Religion of the Renaissance." See A26.

1965

E7.5 "Luther." In *Encyclopedia of the Lutheran Church*, 2:1356–57. Minneapolis: Augsburg, 1965.

1974

E8   "Reformation." In *The New Encyclopedia Britannica Macropoedia.* 15th ed., 15:547–57. Chicago: Encyclopedia Britannica, 1974.

1975

E9   "Calvino." In *Enciclopedia Europea*, vol. 2. Milan: Garzanti, 1975.

1976

E10   "Luther, Martin." In *Collier's Encyclopedia*, 15:111–16. New York: Colliers, 1976 .

1977

E11   "Erasmo." In *Enciclopedia Europea*, vol. 4. Milan: Garzanti, 1977.

1978

E12   "Lutero." In *Enciclopedia Europea*, vol. 7. Milan: Garzanti, 1978.

1979

E13   "Ochino." In *Enciclopedia Europea*, vol. 8. Milan: Garzanti, 1979.

1980

E14   "Serveto." In *Enciclopedia Europea*, vol. 10. Milan: Garzanti, 1980.

F. BOOK REVIEWS

1930

F1   *Luther's Attitude to Religious Liberty*, by W. Köhler. In *Historische Zeitschrift* 141:423.

1931

F2   *God in Freedom: Studies on the Relations between Church and State*, by Luigi Luzzatti. In *Journal of Modern History* 3:287–88.

1932

F3   *The Church in the Roman Empire*, by E. R. Goodenough. In *Church History* 1:127–28.

F4   *History of Later Latin Literature from the Middle of the Fourth to the End of the Seventeenth Century*, by F. A. Wright. In *Church History* 1:182.

F5   *Servet Studies (Bibliographie)*, by W. Köhler. In *Historische Zeitschrift* 146:405.

F6   *St. Philip Neri and the Roman Society of his Times, 1515–1595*, by Louis Ponelle and Louis Bordet. In *American Historical Review* 38:98–100.

1933

F7   *The Two Treatises of Servetus on the Trinity*, by Earl Morse Wilbur. In *Church History* 2:60–61.

1934

F8   *Authority and Reason*, by A. J. MacDonald. In *Church History* 3:82.

F9   *Italy and the Reformation to 1550*, by G. K. Brown. In *American Historical Review* 39:765–66.

F10   *Makers of Christianity from Jesus to Charlemagne*, by Shirley Jackson Case. In *Christian Century* 51:1594–95.

1935

F11   *Tracts on Liberty in the Puritan Revolution*, edited by William Haller. In *Church History* 4:69–70.

1936

F12   *L'Angleterre catholique à la veille du schisme*, by Pierre Janelle. In *American Historical Review* 41:797–98.

F13   *Mistici del duecento e del trecento*, by A. Levasti. In *Church History* 5:389–90.

F14   *Les Origènes de la réforme à Genève*, by Henri Naef. In *Church History* 5:388–89.

1937

F15   *European Civilization: Its Origin and Development*, by various contributors under the direction of Edward Eyre. Vol. 4, *The Reformation*. In *American Historical Review* 42:295–96.

F16   *Franz I. und die Anfänge der französischen Reformation*, by Georg Florial Münzer. In *American Historical Review* 42:86.

F17   *The Historical Scholarship of Saint Bellarmine*, by E. A. Ryan. In *American Historical Review* 43:201.

F18   *The Right to Heresy*, by Stefan Zweig. In *Review of Religion* 1:414–16.

1938

F19   *Christian Hope for World Society*, by John T. McNeill. In *Church History* 7:74–75.

F20   *Consider the Lilies How They Grow*, by John Joseph Stondt. In *Church History* 7:90

F21   *Co-operation or Coercian?*, by L. P. Jacks. In *Yale Divinity News* 34:4–5.

F22   *Menno Simons*, by Cornelius Krahn. In *Church History* 7:199.

F23   *Per la storia degli erectici italiani del secolo XVI in Europa*, testi raccolti da Delio Cantimori et Elisabeth Feist. In *Church History* 7:179–87.

1939

F23.5   *Aktensammlung zur Geschichte der Basler Reformation in den Jahren 1519 bis Anfang 1534*, vol. 3, edited by Paul Roth. In *American Historical Review* 44:706–707.

F24   *Francis Lambert of Avignon*, by R. L. Winters. In *Church History* 7:179–87.

F25   *Das Hochstift Basel im ausgehenden Mittelalter-Quellen und Forschungen*, edited by Konrad W. Hieronimus. In *American Historical Review* 44:706.

F26   *Inquisition and Liberty*, by G. C. Coulton. In *Church History* 8:92.

F27   *Jean Sturm: Classicae epistolae, sive scholae Argentinenses restitutae*, translated and edited by John Rott. In *American Historical Review* 45:216.

F28   *Matricula scholae Argentoratensis, 1621–1721*, translated and edited by John Rott. In *American Historical Review* 45:216.

1940

F29   *La Découverte d'un manuscrit inconnu de Sébastien Castellion*, by Bruno Becker. In *Church History* 9:270–71.

F30   *Eretici italiani del Cinquecento*, by Delio Cantimori. In *Church History* 9:269–70.

F31   *Il Pensiero di Bernadino Ochino*, by Benedetto Nicolini. In *Church History* 9:268–69.

F32   *Per la storia religiosa dello stato di Milano durante il dominio di Carlo V,* by Federico Chabod. In *Church History* 9:267–68.

F33   *The Trial of George Buchanan before the Lisbon Inquisition including the Text of Buchanan's Defense along with Translation and Commentary*, by James M. Aitken. In *American Historical Review* 46:186.

1941

F34   *Criticism of the Crusade*, by P. A. Throop. In *Church History* 10:180–81.

F35   *The Early Tudor Theory of Kingship*, by Franklin L. Baumer. In *Review of Religion* 5:1940–41.

1942

F36   *Aktensammlung zur Geschichte der Basler Reformation in den Jahren 1519 bis Anfang 1534*, vol. 4. *Juli 1529, bis September 1530*, edited by Paul Roth. In *American Historical Review* 47:138.

1943

F37   Introduction to Francesco Patrizi's *Nova de Universis Philosophia*, by Benjamin Brickman. In *Church History*, 12:223–24.

F38   *The Reunion of the Churches: A Study of G. W. Leibniz and His Great Attempt*, by G. J. Jordan. In *The Chronicle* (Protestant Episcopal) 43:5.

1944

F39   *The Fall of Christianity*, by G. J. Heering. In *Christian Century* 61:559–61.

F40   *The Historic Church and Modern Pacifism*, by Humphrey Lee. In *Review of Religion* 8:206–209 and *Fellowship* 10:113–14.

1945

F41   *The Angel of Peace*, by John Amos Comenius. In *Review of Religion* 9:428–29.

F42   *The Christian Interpretation of the Cabala in the Renaissance*, by Joseph Leon Blau. In *Review of Religion* 9:426–27.

F43   *The Church of the Brethren and War*, by Rufus D. Bowman. In *Religion in Life* 14:454–56.

F44   *The Ship of Fools*, by Sebastian Brant. In *Review of Religion* 9:427–28.

F45   *War, Peace, and Non-Resistance*, by Guy F. Hershberger. In *Journal of Religion* 25:303.

1946

F46   *A History of Unitarianism: Socinianism and Its Antecedents*, by Earl Morse Wilbur. In *Review of Religion* 11: 82–84.

F47   *Road to Reformation*, by Heinrich Boehmer. In *Church History* 16:167–76.

F48   *The Saints that Moved the World*, by René Filop-Miller. In *Christendom* 11:276–77.

1947

F49   *The Correspondence of Sir Thomas More*, edited by Elizabeth Rogers. In *Review of Religion*, 12:431–33.

F50   *Le Dottrine politiche da Lutero à Suarez,* by G. Santonastaso. In *Church History* 16:254.

F51   *The Face of the Saints,* by Wilhelm Schamoni. In *Christendom* 12:551–52.

F52   *Melanchthon: Alien or Ally?,* by Franz Hildebrandt. In *American Historical Review* 52:773.

1948

F54   *The English Country Parson,* by William Addison. In *Christendom* 13:404–405.

F55   *Huldrych Zwingli, Band 2, Seine Entwicklung zum Reformation 1520–1575,* by Oscar Farner. In *Theology Today* 5:129–31.

F56   *The World's Great Madonnas,* by Cynthia Pearl Maus. In *Christendom* 13:391–92.

F57   *Die Zusammenarbeit der Renaissancepäpste mit den Türken,* by Hans Pferffermann. In *American Historical Review* 53:321–23.

1949

F58   *The Communion of Saints: A Study of the Origin and Development of Luther's Doctrine of the Church,* by Herman Amberg Preus. In *Interpretation* 3:110–12.

F59   *Contributi alla storia del Concilio di Trento e della Controriforma,* di Eugenio Garin et al. In *Church History* 16:189.

F60   *Evangelische evangelienauslegung,* by Gerhard Ebeling. In *Church History* 18:187.

F61   *Let God Be God,* by Philip S. Watson. In *Theology Today* 6:402–404.

F62   *Lutero,* by G. Miegge. In *Church History* 18:127–28.

F63   *Luther und das Alte Testament,* by Heinrich Bornkamm. In *Church History* 18:125.

F64   *Luthers geistige Welt,* by Heinrich Bornkamm. In *Church History* 18:125.

F65   *Martin Luther der Christenmensch,* by Hans Preus. In *Church History* 18:128.

F66   *Mennonite Piety through the Centuries,* by Robert Friedmann. In *Christian Century* 66:1454–55.

F67   *Die Politisierung des Französischen,* by R. Nürnberger. In *Church History* 18:128.

F68   *Die Reformation in den italienischen Talschaften Graubündens nach dem Briefwechsel Bullingers,* by Peter Dalbert. In *Church History* 18: 188–89.

F69   *The Reinterpretation of Luther, by Edgar M. Carlson.* In *Interpretation* 3:110–12 and *Christian Century* 66:1038–39.

F70   *Theobald Thamer,* by O. Opper. In *Church History* 18:126–27.

F71   *Wittenberg und Byzanz,* by Ernst Benz. In *Church History* 18:126–27.

F72   *The World Student Christian Federation: A History of the First Thirty Years,* by Ruth Rouse. In *Christian Century* 66:683.

1950

F73   *The Admonition Controversy,* by Donald Joseph McGinn. In *Renaissance News* 3:43–44.

F74   *Caspar Schwenckfeld von Ossig,* by Selina Gerhard Schultz. In *Review of Religion* 14:212–13.

F75   *Grundriss zum Studium zur Kirchengeschichte,* by Heinrich Bornkamm. In *Church History* 19:142.

F76   *The Heritage of the Reformation,* by Wilhelm Pauck. In *Theology Today* 7:397–99.

F77   *Inquisitio de Fide, a Colloquy by Erasmus,* translated and edited by Craig R. Thompson. In *Renaissance News* 3:44.

F78   *John Knox's History of the Reformation in Scotland,* edited by William Croft Dickinson. In *Christian Century* 67:924.

F79   *Luther and His Times: The Reformation from a New Perspective,* E. G. Schwiebert. In *Christian Century* 67:1456.

F80   *Wittenberg und Byzanz,* by Ernst Benz. In *Review of Religion* 15:57–60.

1951

F81   *Account of Our Religion, Doctrine and Faith.* Given by Peter Rideman of the Brothers whom Men call Hutterians. Original German Edition 1565. First edition in English translated by Kathleen E. Hasenberg. In *Christian Century* 68:1437–38.

F82   *Great Saints,* by Walter Nigg. In *Review of Religion* 15:57–60.

F83   *Martin Luther und die Reformation im Urteil des deutschen Luthertums: Studien zum Selbstverstandnis des lutherischen Protestantismus von Luthers Tode bis zum Beginn der Goethezeit.I. Band, Darstellung.* In *American Historical Review* 57:150–51.

F84   *Reginald Pole: Cardinal of England,* by W. Schenk. In *American Historical Review* 56:338–39.

1952

F85   *Aktensammlung zur Geschichte der Basler Reformation in den Jahren bis Anfang 1534: VI Band, 1532–1539,* edited by Paul Roth. In *Theology Today* 9:417–18.

F86   *Conrad Grebel, the Founder of the Swiss Brethren,* edited by Harold S. Bender. In *Review of Religion* 16:213–14.

F87   *Democracv and the Churches,* by James Hastings Nichols. In *Theology Today* 9:260–61.

F88   *Geschichte der Reformation und Gegenreformation in den italienischen Südtälern Graubündens und den ehemaligen Untertanenlanden Chiavenna, Veltlin, und Bormio,* by Emil Camenisch. In *Archiv für Reformationsgeschichte* 43:274.

F89   *The Idea of Usury,* by Benjamin N. Nelson. In *Review of Religion* 16:211–13.

F90   *Man and the State,* by Jacques Maritain. In *Political Science Quarterly* 67:27.

F91   *The Right to Heresy: Castellio against Calvin,* by Stefan Zweig. In *Christian Century* 68:19.

F92   *Yale University Portrait Index* 1701–1951. In *Church History* 27:171–72.

1953

F93   *The Anabaptist View of the Church*, by Franklin Hamlin Littell. In *American Historical Review* 58:876–77.

F94   *Bilder und Gestalten aus dem Täufertum*, by W. Wiswedel. In *American Historical Review* 58:876–77.

F95   *History of Christianity, 1650–1950: Secularization of the West*, by James Hastings Nichols. In *Journal of Modern History* 1:56–57.

F96   *Quellen und Forschungen zur Reformationsgeschichte: Quellen zur Geschichte der Widertäufer*. Vol. 13, *Württemberg*, edited by G. Bossert. Vol. 16, *Brandenburg und Bayern: Band I*, edited by K. Schornbaum. Vol. 20, *Glaubenszeugnisse Oberdeutscher Täufgesinnter. Band I*, edited by Lydia Müller. Vol. 13, *Bayern: Band II*, edited by K. Schornbaum. Vol. 24, *Baden-Pfalz*, edited by Manfred Krebs. In *American Historical Review* 58: 875–77.

F97   *Quellen zur Geschichte der Täufer in der Schweiz. Band I, Zürich*, edited by Leonhard von Muralt and Walter Schmid. In *American Historical Review* 58:876–77.

F98   *Studien zur Geschichtsbibel Sebastian Francks*, by Kuno Raber. In *Archiv für Reformationsgeschichte* 44:253–54.

F99   *Urkundliche Quellen zur Hessischen Reformationsgeschichte. Band IV, Wiedertäuferakten 1527–1626*, edited by Walter Koehler, Walter Sohm, Theodor Sippell, and Günther Franz. In *American Historical Review* 58:876–77.

1954

F100   *Advocates of Reform: From Wyclif to Erasmus*, edited by Matthew Spinka. In *American Historical Review* 59:980–81.

F101   *Glaube und Geschichte der Theologie Luthers*, by Hans-Walter Krumweide. In *Journal of Central European Affairs* 14.

F102   *A History of the Ecumenical Movement*, edited by Ruth Rouse and Stephen Charles Neill. In *Ecumenical Review* 6:408–24.

   — Reprinted as chapter 2 of *Collected Papers III*, 24–42, under the title "A Critique of a History of the Ecumenical Movement." See A29.

F103   *Martin Bucers Bedeutung für die europäische Reformationsgeschichte*, by Heinrich Bornkamm. In *Church History* 23:282.

F104   *Puritan Sage: Collected Writings of Jonathan Edwards*, edited by Vergilius Ferm. In *Journal of Religious Thought* 1:2:161–62.

1955

F104.5 *Autour de Michel Servet et de Sébastien Castellion: Recueil*, by Bruno Becker et al. In *Theologische Literaturzeitung* 80:356–58.

F105   *Érasme de Rotterdam et le septième sacrément*, by Émile V. Telle. In *American Historical Review* 60:644–45.

F106   *Forschungen zur Geschichte und Lehre des Protestantismus*, by W. von Loewenich. In *Church History* 24:75.

F107   *Histoire de la tolérance au siècle de la Réforme*. In *Archiv für Reformationsgeschichte* 46:259–60.

F108   *"Landraumig," Sebastian Franck, ein Wanderer an Donau, Rhein, und Neckar*, by Eberhard Teufel. In *American Historical Review* 60:964.

F109   *Die Motivering van de Godsdienstvrijheid bij Dirck Volckertszoon Coornhert*, by Hendrik Bonger. In *American Historical Review* 60:964.

F110   *The Prophetic Faith of Our Fathers*, by LeRoy Edwin Frome. In *Theology Today* 12:400–401.

F111   *Recherches sur l'imprimerie à Genève de 1550–1564*, by Paul Chaix. In *Archiv für Reformationsgeschichte* 46:275.

F112   *Das Selbstzeugnis Kaiser Konstantins*, by Hermann Dörries. In *Church History* 24:71–72.

F113   *William of Hornes, Lord of Heze and the Revolt of the Netherlands (1576–1580)*, by Gordon Griffiths. In *Archiv für Reformationsgeschichte* 46:278–79.

F114   *Foundation of American Freedom*, by A. Mervyn Davies. In *American Historical Review* 61:729.

F115   *Jacopo Aconcio. Traduzione di Delio Cantimori*, by Charles D. O'Malley. In *Church History* 25:87–88.

F116   *Luther*, by Rudolf Thiel. In *The Pastor* (April): 40.

F117   Puritanism in Old and New England, by Alan Simpson. In American Academy of Political and Social Sciences 305:181.

F118   Schriften, by Hans Denck. 1. Teil. Bibliographie, edited by Georg Baring. In Archiv für Reformationsgeschichte 47:277–78.

1957

F118.5 Bibliographie des oeuvres d'Estienne Pesquier, by D. Thickett. In Archiv für Reformations geschichte 48:1:138–39.

F119   Byzantine Background to the Italian Renaissance, by K. M. Setton. In Church History 26:386.

F120   The Christian Scholar in the Age of the Reformation, by E. Harris Harbison. In American Historical Review 62:612–13.

F121   The Complete Writings of Menno Simons, edited by John Christian Wenger. In Theology Today 8:565–66.

F122   De Spiritu Sanctu: Der Beitrag des Basilius zum Abschluss des trinitarischen Dogmas, by Hermann Dörries. In Church History 26:384–85.

F123   Épitres du coq à l'âne, by Henri Meylan. In Church History 26:384–85.

F124   Mennonite Encyclopedia, vol. 1. In Church History 26:294.

F124.5 Philosophy of the Church Fathers, vol. 1: Faith, Trinity, Incarnation, by Harry Austryn Wolfson. In Journal of Religious Thought 14:71–72.

F125   The Reformation: A History of European Civilization from Wyclif to Calvin, 1300–1564. (The Story of Civilization 4), by Will Durant. In Herald Tribune Book Review 29 (September): 3.

1958

F126   Aspects de la propagande religieuse, by G. Berthoud et al. In American Historical Review 63:654–55.

F127   Au coeur religieuse du XVI siècle, by Lucien Febvre. In American Historical Review 63:1049–50.

F128   Christianity in a Revolutionary Age, by Kenneth Scott Latourette. In The Nineteenth Century. In Yale Divinity News (November): 9.

F129   *The Development of the German Public Mind: A Social History of German Political Sentiments, Aspirations, and Ideas*, by Frederick Hertz. In *Political Science Quarterly* 73:160.

F130   *Landgraf Philipp und die Toleranz: Ein christlicher Fürst der linke Flügel, der Reformation und christlicher Primitivismus*, by Franklin Hamlin Littell. In *Journal of Ecclesiastical History* 9:126–27.

F130.5   *Puritanism in the Period of the Great Persecution 1660–1688*, by Gerald R. Cragg. In *Religion and Life* 27:315–16.

F131   *The Reverend Jonathan Lee and the 18th Century Township of Salisbury, Ct.*, by Julia Pettee. In *ATLA* [American Theological Library Association] *Newsletter* 5:14.

1959

F131.5   *Socinianism in Poland: The Social and Political Ideas of the Polish Antitrinitarians in the 16th and 17th Centuries*, by Stanislaw Kot. In *Journal of Religion* 38:206–207.

F132   *Martin Luther and the Luther Film of 1953*, by Albert Hyma. In *American Historical Review* 64:380.

F133   *New Light on Martin Luther, with an Authentic Account of the Luther Film of 1953*, by Richard M. Douglas. In *American Historical Review* 64: 380–81.

F134   *Pictorial History of Protestantism*, by Vergilius Ferm. In *Archiv für Reformationsgeschichte* 50:191–92.

F135   *Religion and Learning at Yale: The Church of Christ in the College and University, 1757–1957*, by Ralph Henry Gabriel. In *Yale Divinity News* (January): 13.

F135.5   *The Revolt of Martin Luther*, by Robert Herndon Fife. In *Interpretation* 12:373–74.

F136   *Schriften*, by Hans Denck. *2. Teil. Religiöse Schriften*, edited by Walter Fellmann. In *Archiv für Reformationsgeschichte* 50:120.

F137   *Sebastian Castellio*, by H.R. Guggisberg. In *Church History* 28:106.

F137.5   *The History of the Christian Church*, by Williston Walker. In *Union Seminary Quarterly Review* 15:56–58.

F138 *Young Man Luther: A Study in Psychoanalysis and History,* by Erik Erikson. In *Yale Review* 48: 405–10.

— Reprinted in *Collected Papers II,* 86–90, under the title "Luther's Life in Review. II. A Critique of Erik H. Erikson's Young Man Luther." See A28.

1960

F139 *Concordia Mundi,* by W. J. Bouwsma. In *Church History* 29:104–105.

F141 *A History of Modern Germany: The Reformation,* by Hajo Holborn. In *Church History* 29:100–101.

F142 *Jacopo Sadoleto, 1477–1547: Humanist and Reformer,* by Richard M. Douglas. In *American Historical Review* 65:424–25

F143 *Juan de Valdés y el pensamiento religioso europeo en los siglos XVI y XVII,* by Domingo Ricart. In *Renaissance News* 8:153–54.

F144 *The Learned Men,* by Gustavus S. Paine. In *Saturday Review* 43:27.

F145 *Das Werden des Neuzeitlichen Europa 1300–1600,* by Erich Hassinger. In *Journal of Modern History* 32:270–71.

1961

F145.5 *Franz Lambert von Avignon und die Reformation in Hessen,* by Gerhard Müller. In *American Historical Review* 66:522.

F146 *Ginevra e l'Italia: Raccolta di studi promossa dalla Facolta Valdese di Teologia di Roma,* edited by Delio Cantimori et alii. In *American Historical Review* 66:1100–1101.

F147 *Hutterite Studies: Festschrift,* by R. F. Friedmann. In *Church History* 31:246–47.

F148 *Pietro Giannone: riformatore e storico,* by Brunello Vigezzi. In *American Historical Review* 67:208–209.

F149 *A Reformation Paradox,* by Kenneth A. Strand. In *Renaissance News* 14:105–106.

F150 *Toleration and the Reformation,* by Joseph Lecler. In *American Historical Review* 66:1011–13

1962

F150.5   *Hutterite Studies: Essays by Robert Friedmann Collected and Published in Honor of his 70th Anniversary,* edited by H. S. Bender. In *Church History* 32:246–47.

F150.6   *Institutes of the Christian Religion,* by John Calvin, 2 vols. translated by F. L. Battles and J. T. McNeill. In *Interpretation* 16:98–100.

F151   *The Two Reformations in the Sixteenth Century: A Study of the Religious Aspects and Consequences of Renaissance and Humanism,* by H. A. van Gelder. In *American Historical Review* 68:81–82.

1963

F152   *The Heritage of the Reformation,* by Wilhelm Pauck. In *Theologische Literaturzeitung* 88:438.

F153   *Islam,* by George Hunston Williams. In *Religious Education* 58:310–12.

F154   *Luther und die Welt des 20. Jahrhunderts.* In *Theologische Literaturzeitung* 88:438.

F155   *Makers of Religious Freedom in the Seventeenth Century: Samuel Rutherford, Alexander Henderson, John Bunyan, Richard Baxter,* by Marcus L. Loane. In *Christian Century* 80:50–51.

F156   *The Religious Renaissance of the German Humanists,* by Lewis W. Spitz. In *American Historical Review* 69:127–28.

F157   *Der Späte Erasmus und die Reformation,* by Karl Heinz Oelrich. In *Archiv für Reformationsgeschichte* 54:271–72.

1964

F158   *Christianity on the March,* edited by Henry P. Van Dusen. In *Church History* 33:503.

F158.5   *Creeds of the Churches: A Reader in Christian Doctrine from the Bible to the Present,* by John H. Leith. In *Journal for the Scientific Study of Religion* 4:122–23.

F159   *Millenial Dreams in Action: Essays in Comparative Study,* edited by Sylvia Thrupp. In *American Church History* 69:1106–1107.

F160   *Registres de la compagnie des pasteurs de Genève au temps de Calvin,* published by Robert M. Kingdon and J. F. Bergier. In *Archiv für Reformationsgeschichte* 55:279–80.

F161   *Die Schule bei Martin Bucer in ihrem Verhältnis zu Kirche und Obrigkeit,* by Ernst-Wilhelm Kohls. In *Church History* 33:221–22.

F162   *Worship and Theology in England: From Newman to Martineau, 1850–1900,* by Horton Davies. In *Church History* 33:107–108.

1965

F163   *Christianity and History: Essays,* by E. Harris Harbison. In *American Historical Review* 70:1148–49.

F163.5 *The English Reformation,* by Arthur Geoffrey Dickens. In *Journal of Ecclesiastical History* 16:243–44.

F164   *A History of the Reformation,* by John P. Dolan. In *Commonweal* 83:65–67.

F164.5 *Luther's World of Thought,* by Heinrich Bornkamm. Translated by M. H. Bertram. In *Theologische Literaturzeitung* 92:688.

F165   *Schriften,* by Hans Denck. *3. Teil. Exegetische Schriften Gedichte und Briefe,* edited by Pastor Walter Fellmann. In *Archiv für Reformationsgeschichte* 55:279–80.

1966

F165.5 *Henry VIII and the Lutherans: A Study in Anglo-Lutheran Relations from 1521–1547,* by Neelok Serawlook Tjernagel. In *Journal of Church and State* 8:460–61.

F166   *Naissance et affirmation de la Réforme,* by Jean Delumeau. In *American Historical Review* 71:511.

F166.5 *Das Zeugnis der Reformation,* by Willem Hendrik van de Pol. Translated by B. and G. Rosenmollet. In *Journal of Ecumenical Studies* 3:196–97.

1967

F167   *Die Einziehung des geistlichen Gutes im albertinische Sachsen, 1539–1553,* by Helga-Maria Kuhn. In *American Historical Review* 73:510–11.

F170   *Die Theologie des Erasmus,* by *Ernst-Wilhelm Kohls.* In *Church History* 36:222–23.

1968

F171   *Francisco de Ossuna, Mystik und Rechtfortigung,* by Hans-Jürgen Prien. In *Church History* 37:338.

F171.5 *Geneva and the Consolidation of the French Protestant Movement 1564–1572,* by Robert M. Kingdon. In *Journal of Religious History* 5:75–76.

F172   *The Impact of the Church upon Its Culture: Reappraisals of the History of Christianity,* by Quirinus Breen et al. In *American Historical Review* 74:540–41.

F173   *Reformata Reformanda. Festgabe für Hubert Jedin zum 17. juni 1965,* edited by Erwin Iserloh and Konrad Repgen. In *Archiv für Reformationsgeschichte* 59:102–106.

F174   *Reich und Reformation,* by Stephen Skalwert. In *American Historical Review* 73:1552–53.

F174.5 *Religion and Regime: A Sociological Account of the Reformation,* by Guy E. Swanson. In *Journal of Church and State* 10:445–47.

F175   *The Spirit of the Counter-Reformation: The Birkbeck Lectures in Ecclesiastical History given in the University of Cambridge in May, 1951,* by H. Outram Evennett. In *American Historical Review* 74: 579–80.

F176   *Die Stellung des Erasmus von Rotterdam zur Römischer Kirche,* by Georg Gebhardt. In *Archiv für Reformationsgeschichte* 59:249–50.

1969

F177   *The English Presbyterians from Elizabethan Puritanism to Modern Unitarianism,* by C. Gordon Bolam et al. In *Church History* 38:123–24.

F177.5 *Interpreters of Luther: Essays in Honor of Wilhelm Pauck,* edited by Jaroslav J. Pelikan. In *Religion in Life* 38:2.

1970

F178   *Camillo Renato, opere documenti e testimonianze,* edited by Antonio Rotondò. In *Journal of Modern History* 42:649–50.

F179 *In Defense of Martin Luther,* by John Warwick Montgomery. In *Fides et Historia* (1970): 79–80.

F181 *Pacifism in the United States from the Colonial Era to the First World War,* by Peter Brock. In *Church History* 39:127–28.

1971

F181.5 *Bucer and Erasmus,* by Friedhelm Krüger. In *Lutheran World* 18:85–86.

F182 *Ein Klag des Frydens by Erasmus,* translated by Leo Jed. In *Erasmus: Speculum Scientarum* 23:210.

F183 *Il Nicodemismo: Simulazione e dissimulazione religiosa nell'Europa del 500,* by Carlo Ginzburg. In *Journal of Modern History* 43:309–11.

F184 *To End War: A History of the National Council for the Prevention of War,* by Frederick J. Libby. In *Fellowship* (March): 22.

F184.5 *Young Man Luther,* by Erik H. Erikson. In *Religion in Life* 40:450, 478.

1972

F184.6 *Church History in an Age of Science,* by Henry W. Bowden. In *Religion in Life* 41:286–87.

F185 *Erasmus and the Seamless Robe of Jesus: De Sarcienda Ecclesiae Concordia (On Restoring the Unity of the Christian Church) with Selections from the Letters and Ecclesiastes,* edited by Raymond Himelick. In *Review of Books and Religion* (May): 5.

F186 *Philologie und praktische philosophie,* by Dietrich Harth. In *Erasmus: Speculum Scientarum* 24:644–45.

F186.5 *La Riforma protestante,* by Valdo Vinay. In *Church History* 41:122.

1973

F187 *Chemins de l'hérésie: Textes et documents,* vol. 2, by Eugénie Droz. In *Journal of Modern History* 45:299.

F188 *De l'impunité des hérétiques: "De Haereticis non Puniendis,"* by Sébastien Castellion. Unedited Latin text by Bruno Becker. Published in French by M. Valkhoff. In *Journal of Modern History* 45:299.

F189   *Pietro Bizzarri esule italiano del Cinquecento,* by Massimo Firpo. In *Journal of Modern History* 45:486.

F189.5   *Schism, Heresy, and Religious Protest,* edited by Derek Baker. In *Church History* 42:275–76.

1974

F189.9   *Julius Pflug, Correspondence,* edited by J.V. Pollet. In *Church History* 43:402–403.

F190   *"Mystère" et "Philosophie du Christ" selon Érasme: Étude de la lettre à Paul Volz et de la "Ratio" verae theologiae (1518),* by Georges Chantraine. In *American Historical Review* 79:1536–37.

1975

F191   *Luther,* by Richard Marius. In *Christian Century* 92:173–75.

F192   *Medieval Aspects of Renaissance Learning,* by Paul Oskar Kristeller. In *Renaissance Quarterly* 28:229–30.

F193   *Trumpeter of God: A Biography of John Knox,* by W. Stanford Reid. In *American Historical Review* 80:1340.

F194   *Werke,* by Heinrich Bullinger. (Several parts by various editors), in *American Historical Review* 80:1004–1005.

1977

F195   *Christian Art in Asia,* by Masao Takenaka. In *Theology Today* 34:98–102.

F196   *Theology, Reason and the Limitations of War: Religion and Secular Concepts, 1200–1740,* by James Turner Johnson. In *American Political Science Review* 71:1136–37.

1978

F197   *Action and Person: Conscience in Late Scholasticism and the Young Luther,* by Michael G. Baylor. In *American Historical Review* 83:185–86.

F198   *Frank Chamberlain Porter, Pioneer in American Biblical Interpretation and Benjamin Wisner Bacon, Pioneer in American Biblical Criticism,* by Roy A. Harrisville. In *Reflection* 7:12.

1979

F199   *Erasmus in het Nederlands tot 1617*, by Simon Wellem Bijl. In *Renaissance Quarterly* 32:209–11.

F200   *Erasmus on Language and Method in Theology*, by Marjorie O'Rourke Boyle. In *Renaissance Quarterly* 32:100–101.

1980

F200.5   *Luther's House of Learning: Indoctrination of the Young in the German Reformation*, by Gerald Strauss. In *Church History* 49:86–87.

1981

F200.7   *Restitucion del Cristianismo*, by Miguel Servet. In *Renaissance Quarterly* 34 (Winter 1981): 583–84.

1982

F201   *Die Reformation als Problem der amerikanischen Historiographie*, by Ulrich Michael Kremer. In [source unknown] 107 (May 1982): 363–65.

1984

F202   *Luther*, by Richard Marius. In *Christian Century* 101: 692–93.

G. INTRODUCTIONS AND FOREWORDS
TO THE WORKS OF OTHERS

1953

G1   Introduction to *Autour de Michel Servet et de Sébastien Castellion*, edited by Bruno Becker. Haarlem: H. D. Tjeenk Willenk, 1953 .

1964

G2   Foreword to *The Quakers in Puritan England*, by Hugh Stewart Barbour. New Haven: Yale University Press, 1964 (Yale Publications in Religion).

1965

G3   Introduction to *Hutterite Life*, by John Andrew Hostetler. Scottdale, Pa.: Herald Press, 1965.

G4   Prologo to *Historia del pensamiento cristiano*, by Justo L. González. Buenos Aires: Methopress, 1965 (Biblioteca de estudios teologicos).

1969

G5   Foreword to *Strangers and Exiles: A History of Religious Refugees*, by Frederick A. Norwood. Vol. 1. Nashville: Abingdon, 1969.

1970

G5.5   Foreword to *A History of Christian Thought*, vol. 1. *From the Beginnings to the Council of Chalcedon*, by Justo L. González. Nashville: Abingdon, 1970.

1975

G6   "A Word of Introduction" to *Inquisitio de Fide: A Colloquy*, by Desiderius Erasmus Rotterdamus, 1524. Edited by Craig R. Thompson. Hamden, Ct.: Archon Books, 1975.

1980

G7   *Introduction to The Golden Years of the Hutterites: The Witness and Thought of the Communal Moravian Anabaptists during the Walpot Era, 1565–1578*, by Leonard Gross. Scottsdale, Pa.: Herald Press, 1980.

1982

G8　　Foreword to *German Humanism and Reformation*, edited by Reinhard P. Becker. New York: Continuum, 1982.

H. POETRY

1979

H1　　"The Nativity" and "Antonimies," in *Currrents in Theology and Mission* 6:6 (December 1979): 325.

Christmas card sent by Roland H. Bainton, 1982.

I. WORDS FOR MUSIC

Roland Bainton's translation of Martin Luther's *Von Himmel Hoch, da Komm' Ich Her* appeared as lyrics for music in several places including those cited below. The text first appeared in *The Martin Luther Christmas Book* (1948). See A10.

1959

I1   *From Heaven High I Come to Earth*. Words from Martin Luther, translated by Roland Bainton. Setting by Healey Willan after *Von Himmel Hoch*. "Geistlichelieder, Leipzig, 1939. In *Carols of the Seasons*. St. Louis: Concordia Publishing House, 1959.

1963

I2   *From Heaven High I Come to Earth*. A Christmas cantata for two-part choir, soloists, congregation, oboe, violin, organ, and violincello ad libitum. Music by Jan Bender. Opus 27. Words by Martin Luther, translated by Roland H. Bainton. St. Louis: Concordia Publishing House, 1963.

I3   *From Heaven on High I Come to Earth*. English translation of text of Martin Luther's Christmas Hymn written for his children in 1534. Eight of the original fifteen stanzas printed in *Christian Hymns*, edited by Luther Noss. New York: World Publishing Co., 1963.

1964

I4   *Lord God, Thy Name We Praise*. Translated from the Latin *Te Deum Laudamus* by Roland H. Bainton using Martin Luther's 1529 metrical version and Bach harmonisations. Sung in Battell Chapel, Yale University on Reformation Sunday, 25 October 1964.

1967

I5   *From Heaven High I Come to Earth*. Christmas cantata for soprano or tenor soloist, children or young people, and unison choir with congregation. Accompaniment for organ (or piano), trumpet, and several solo instruments. English text by Roland H. Bainton. Music by H. LeRoy Baumgartner. Opus 96. Based on the folk song melody "In thun wie man umb krenze singt" and the chorale tune "Von Himmel Hoch der komm ich her." Springfield, Ohio: Chantry Press at Wittenberg University, 1967.

J. PUBLISHED DRAWINGS AND PAINTINGS

A sketch pad and pencil were constant companions for RHB. His caricatures and drawings have delighted many, including those who often unwittingly became his subjects, over many years. His travels usually resulted in collections of watercolors produced from sketches which recorded both important events and local color in everyday life. Unpublished sketches and watercolors go far beyond what is listed here. (Some are included in the Roland H. Bainton Papers at Yale Divinity School Library. A listing from the Register of the Papers can be found in this bibliography (see R1). RHB's artwork was an important and distinctive part of his life and work.

ILLUSTRATIONS FOR HIS OWN BOOKS

The author adapted existing illustrative material for use in his own works. He also created original sketches included in the publications listed below.

J1   *The Church of Our Fathers.* See A7. See also pp. xii–xiii of this work.

J2   *The Covenant in the Wilderness: The New Haven Green in 1815.*

          — The cover of this work shows an adaptation of old prints of the Yale campus. See A15.

J2.5   *The Douglas Clyde Macintosh Fellowship in Theology and the Philosophy of Religion.* See A21.5.

          — Cover illustration by RHB.

J3   *The Panorama of the Christian Church in Kodachrome Slides.*

          — RHB painted some of the slides in this set including no. 150, "The Edinburgh Conference." See A9.

J3.5   *Pilgrim Parson: The Life of James Herbert Bainton, 1867–1942.* See A21.

J4   *Roly.* See A39.

J5   *Vignettes of Men Memorialized in the Buildings of the Yale Divinity School.* See A19.

J5.5   *Yale and the Ministry: A History of Education for the Christian Ministry at Yale from the Founding in 1701.* See A20.

Sterling Divinity Triangle, Yale University, by Roland H. Bainton.

YALE SOURCES

J6   *1960 Class Letter.* Yale Divinity School Class of 1955. Issue no. 4. 1958–60.

    — Cover by RHB depicting Sterling Quadrangle and Marquand Chapel.

J7   *Reflection.* Yale Divinity School.

    — "Caricature of George Pierson" (November 1966): 11.

    — "Caricature of Modern Art" (November 1968): 3.

    — "Caricature of Reflection" (May 1970): cover.

George Pierson,
by RHB

    — "Sketches of the Faculty" (May 1973): several pages.

    — "Drawing of Liston Pope" (March 1974): 8.

J8   *Student Directory—Yale University Divinity School, 1969–1970.*

"The cover sketch was done by Professor Roland Bainton and was taken from the crufixion on the doors of St. Paul's Church in Ebutte, Meta, Lagos, Nigeria. According to Professor Bainton, there is a striking similarity between this representation of the crufixion and that used by the earlier Christians in the 5th century A.D."

J9   *Yale Divinity News*

    — "Sketch of Millar Burrows" (May 1958): 11.

    — Caricatures of nineteenth-century Preacher Hubert Greaves and Yale's Professor of Homiletics, William Muehl. (March 1959): 7.

    — Sketches of Joseph Sittler, Wilhelm Pauck, and Timothy Dwight the Younger on the occasion of the Beecher and Taylor Lectures. (May 1959): 11, 20)

Joseph Sittler,
by RHB

    — "Sketches from the Versatile Pen of Roland Bainton: Halford Luccock" (November 1959): 9.

— "Sketches from the Versatile Pen of Roland Bainton: Clarence Shedd" (March 1960): 7.

— Sketch of Robert Calhoun. (May 1965): 3.

J10   *Yale Historical Bulletin.*

— Caricature of Harry R. Rudin, Chairman of the History Department, 1952–summer 1956. (March 1957): 4.
  Caption: "Thou shalt not make unto thee any graven images, or…bow down thyself to them, nor serve them. (From the Gospel of the Professors, as illustrated in the Book of Bainton."

— Caricature of Ralph H. Gabriel, History Department. (April 1958): 4.
  On the occasion of his retirement. Caption: "Ralph Gabriel at the beginning of his teaching career in 1918."

Ralph Gabriel,
by RHB

— Caricature of R. S. Lopez, History Department. (April 1959): 4.
  Caption: "Italy over Two Thousand Years: R. S. Lopez according to Roland Bainton."

— Caricature of Professor Guber. (April 1959): 12.
  Caption: "Professor Guber of the I.C.H.S."

— Caricature of Frank L. Baumer, History Department.
  Caption: FLB at a Doctoral Examination (as seen by fellow sufferer, RHB."

— Self-caricature. 20 (1962): 14.

OTHER SOURCES

J11   *Bond* (Lutheran Brotherhood) (October 1975): 4.

— Includes several small sketches from a visit to Japan in an article by Herbert Brokering. See O12.

— These sketches were reproduced from a much larger collection published in *Japanese Christian Quarterly.* See J15.

J12   *Commonweal* (17 September 1971): 20 and (15 October 1971): 3.

— Earlier citation is a cover woodcut illustration.

— Later citation was taken from The *Church of Our Fathers.* See A7.

J13   Froude, Anthony. *The Cat's Pilgrimage: A Fable by James Anthony Froude.*
New Haven: East Rock Press, 1949.

— Illustrations by RHB.

J14   *Harvard Magazine* (May 1975): 52.

"A Portrait of Professor Henry Joel Cadbury drawn by
Roland Bainton, a Yale professor, in 1947. Cadbury was
then in Oslo to accept the Nobel Peace Prize on behalf of
the American Friends Service Committee."

— Caption: "Nobel Oblige."

Henry Cadbury,
by RHB

J15   *Japanese Christian Quarterly* (spring 1968): 104–12.

— A collection of sketches made on a visit to Japan.

J16   *Journal of Presbyterian History* (fall 1973): 251–66.

"Churchmen à la Roland Bainton."

— Sketches of Presbyterian and Reformed
churchmen including H. Richard Niebuhr,
Charles H. Forman, William Sloane Coffin,
Jr., Henry Pitney Van Dusen, Reinhold Nie-
buhr, James Moffat, Robert Hastings
Nichols, Karl Barth, Emil Brunner.

J17   *In Context* (spring 1953): 24–25.

— "Sketches from *The Mikado*"

H. Richard Niebuhr,
by RHB

J18   *Karl Barth and the Future of Theology.* A
Memorial Colloquium Held at the Yale
Divinity School. 28 January 1969, edited by David L. Dickerman.

— Cover entitled "Caricature of Karl Barth" by RHB.

J19   *Monthly Newsletter.* Foundation for Reformation Research, no. 13 (January
1968).

— Sketches made at a board meeting of Ron Diener, Edgar Carlson, Harold Grimm, Conrad Frey, Oswald Hoffman, Robert Kingdon, and Carl Meyer.

J20   *New Haven Register.* (28 February 1971): 20, 22 and (25 May 1975): sec. A, 10.

— Earlier citation includes two watercolors appearing in an article by John Knoble depicting Yale students. See O21.

— Later citation is a drawing of a car on a Polish street. See O21.

J21   *Register-Leader.* (midsummer 1966): 3.

— Caricature of James Luther Adams.

— Appears with article by Adams entitled "Hits Wing Ball Games: Power in Creative Controversy."

J22   *Unitarian Register* (midsummer 1959): 404.

— Caption: "The Bandstand in Boston Common is a landmark to May meetings visitors."

J23   Tappert, Helen Carson. *The Reflective Reformer; Theodore G. Tappert: Teacher, Historian, and Theologian.* Philadelphia: Y Press, 1977.

— Caricature of Tappert.

J24   *Waiilatpu* (Whitman College Yearbook, vol. 7). Menasha, Wisc.: George Banta Publishing Company for the Collegiate Press, 1913.

— Caricatures of professors made into birds, 244–48.

— Clay sculpture caricatures, 262.

— Foreword by Paul Willard Garrett expresses debt to Roland Bainton, '14, "for his extraordinary clay and caricature work."

J25   *Religion in the Schools.* A Publication of the Council for Religion in Independent Schools. n.d.

— Sketch entitled "The Berkeley Center."

OTHER PRINTED DRAWINGS AND PAINTINGS

J26   *Holden Village Publications*
        Roland Bainton often spent time at this Lutheran retreat center in the
        Cascade Mountains near Lake Chelan in the state of Washington.

        — *Holden Village Calendar,* 1968.
        July/August and September feature two landscape watercolors.
        Includes a biographical sketch of RHB, who was a faculty member
        in the Village in 1967.

        — *Holden Village Courier,* 1968.
        Nine sketches scattered throughout the issue.

        — "Sketch of Holden Village in Red" (August 1971).
        Used in poster advertisement for Holden Village, 1972.

        — "Sketch of Holden Village in Brown" (August 1971).
        Used in advertising brochure for Holden Village, 1972.
        Caption: "Dr. Roland Bainton gives us his impression of a day in
        Holden."

        — "Caricatures in Color of Holden Village" (1970).
        This file of 15 different sketches was found among the author's
        papers. It is uncertain which of the sketches may have been used by
        Holden Village.

J27   *The Mercury* (Gettysburg College). 75th Anniversary Edition (spring
        1968): 22.
        Two caricatures.
        Caption: "Former Presidents Hanson and Paul when receiving
        honorary doctorates at Gettysburg in 1958."

J28   *Reformation Day: 1517–1952: A Service of Worship for the Renewal of Protes-*
        tant Witness (31 October 1952).

        — "The illustrated cover and the service of worship for Reformation
        Day, 1953, were prepared by Professor Roland H. Bainton, the Divin-
        ity School, Yale University, for the Department of Worship and the
        Fine Arts, National Council of Churches."

J29   *Tamiment Chamber Music Festival.* 24–27 June 1954. (Tamiment in-the-
        Poconos, Tamiment, Pa.)

        — Cover by RHB taken from a sixteeth-century woodcut.

K. RECORDS, TAPES, SLIDES, AND FILMS

1944–45

K1   *The Panorama of the Christian Church in Kodachrome Slides.*

— See A9 and J3.

1954

K1.2   *Freedom's Religious Foundations.* New York: National Council of the Churches of Christ in the United States of America. 1 sound cassette (42 min.), analog. 1-7/8 ips. Mono.

— Address recorded at the 3rd Assembly of the National Council, Boston, Mass., 1 November.

K1.3   *The New England Way.* Berkeley, Ca.: Pacific School of Religion, 1954. 3 sound recordings.

— E. T. Earle Lectures, 1954. Recorded 23–25 February in Berkeley.

— Includes 3 presentations: (1) "Jonathan Edwards and the Great Awakening," (2) "Nathaniel Taylor and the New Haven Theology," (3) "Horace Bushnell and Emergent Liberalism."

196–

K1.5   *Luther's Bible Meditations in Sound Recording.* New Haven: Yale Divinity School Visual Education Service. 1 sound cassette. 1-7/8 ips. 2 track. Mono.

K1.6   Luther's Christmas Sermon (side one) and Interview with Roland Bainton on the topic "Why Study Erasmus?" New Haven: Yale Divinity School Visual Education Service. 1 sound cassette. 1-7/8 ips. 2-track. Mono

K1.7   *On War and Peace.* New Haven: Yale Divinity School Visual Education Service. 1 sound cassette. 1-7/8 ips. 2 track. Mono.

— Recorded on both sides.

1960

K1.8   *1960 Cole Lectures.* Delivered before Vanderbilt University Divinity School. 7 sound cassettes. 17/8 ips. 3 7/8 x 2 1/2 in.

— Title taken from label on cassette.

— Unpublished lectures.

1962

K2   *Martin Luther Christmas Sermon* and *Pictures of Jesus.* 12" LP record.

— Available from Yale Divinity School in May 1962

— Mentioned in *New Haven Register* article, 1 July 1962. See O21.

1967

K3   *Erasmus and the Strategy of Mediation.* Princeton, N.J.: Princeton Theological Seminary Speech Studios. 5 cassettes. 2-track, mono. (75 min. each)

— Five Lectures in the Stone Lecture Series delivered at Princeton Theological Seminary, 6–8 February.

— Part of "The Listening Library."

K3.4   *[Erasmus].* 1 sound tape reel. 3 3/4 ips. 7 in.

— Lecture delivered at the University of Chattanooga, Tennessee 16 November.

— Title supplied by cataloger.

K3.5   *[Martin Luther and the Reformation].* 1 sound tape reel. 3 3/4 ips. 7 in.

— Lecture delivered at the University of Chattanooga, Tennessee, 17 November.

— Title supplied by cataloger.

1968

K3.6   *Christmas Sermon* by Martin Luther on Phonotape. 1 reel. 3 3/4 ips. 1-track. 7 in.

— Compiled by RHB from thirty-six years of Luther's Christmas sermons.

— Given at Holden Village, Chelan, Washington, probably during the summer of 1968.

K3.7   *Erasmus.* New Haven: Yale Divinity School Visual Education Service, [1968]. 2 sound cassettes. 1-7/8 ips. 2 track. Mono.

— Recorded in November at the Ecumenical Continuing Education Center.

— Recorded on both sides.

K3.8   *Erasmus and the Liberal Catholic Reform.* 1 sound cassette (52 min). analog. 1-7/8 ips. Mono.

— "Erasmus and Reform," Lecture 1.

— Alumni lecture recorded at Union Theological Seminary, Richmond, Virginia, 5 March.

K3.9   *Erasmus and the Protestant Reform.* 1 sound cassette (60 min). analog. 1-7/8 ips. Mono.

— "Erasmus and Reform," Lecture 2.

— Alumni lecture recorded at Union Theological Seminary, Richmond, Virginia, 6 March.

1969

K4   *Martin Luther and the Reformation.* New Haven: Yale Divinity School Visual Education Service. 1 sound cassette. 1-7/8 ips. 2 track. Mono.

— Lecture delivered at the Ecumenical Continuing Education Center.

K4.3   "Reformation Then and Now," for *Luther Legacy: Twelve Classics of Martin Luther's Message and Eighteen Hymns of Martin Luther.*

Sponsored by the Lutheran ministers of greater New Haven. With the Schola Moderna Chorale, early instruments, organ, and members of the New York Brass Quintet. (A Schola Moderna Recording. XSV 124882. Stereo. 4 sides. 12" phonodiscs.)

— RHB's commentary is found on the slipcase.

197–

K4.4   *A History of Women at YDS.* New Haven: Yale Divinity School. 2 sound cassettes.

[101]

K4.5   *An Interview.* Tape-recorded interview conducted by Parker Rossman. Waco, Tex.: Creative Resources.

K4.6   *Martin Luther Christmas Sermon.* New Haven: Yale Divinity School. 1 sound cassette. analog. 1-7/8 ips. Mono.

— RHB read Martin Luther's Christmas sermon and commented on its simplicity and style for its day.

K4.7   *Pictures of Christ.* (New Haven: Yale Divinity School). 1 sound cassette (20 min). analog. 1-7/8 ips. Mono

— Recorded sermon. RHB discussed representations of Jesus in art and literature.

K4.8   *The Story of Yale Divinity School.* New Haven: Yale Divinity School Visual Education Service. 1 sound cassette. (60 min). 1-7/8 ips. 4 track. Mono.

— Lecture on the history of Yale Divinity School from 1701–1900. Biographical sketches of selected teaching faculty members.

K4.9   *Women of the Reformation.* New Haven: Yale Divinity School Visual Education Service. 1 sound cassette. analog. Mono.

1970

K5   *Erasmus.* Hickory, N.C.: Lenoir-Rhyne College. 2 sound cassettes. (70 min). 1-7/8 ips. analog. Mono.

— Recorded on November 5.

K5.1   *The Worst Century.* Richmond, Va.: Union Theological Seminary. 1 sound cassette. (40 min). 1-7/8 ips. analog. Mono.

— Baccalaureate sermon, 17 May. Based on text from Rev. 6:12–17, 21:1–5 concerning eschatology.

1971

K5.5   *The Reformation.* Phonotape. Waco, Tex.: Creative Resources. CRC.

— Includes program notes and five-page discussion guide.

1972

K5.7   *The Reformation.* Waco, Tex.: Creative Resources. 4 sound cassettes. (364 min.) 1-7/8 ips.

— With accompanying pamphlet, 36 pages, 2 x 22 cm. Discovery series.

K6   *Roland Bainton.* St. Paul: Minnesota Public Radio, A373. 1 cassette. 2-track. Mono. Broadcast late 1972.

1974

K7   *Alumni Address,* February 1974. New Haven, Ct.: Yale Divinity School Visual Education Service. 1 sound cassette.

K7.1   *Behold the Christ.* New Haven: Yale Divinity School Visual Education Service. 1 sound cassette (60 min). 1-7/8 ips. 4 track. Mono.

— Address concerning events and themes in the life of Jesus Christ and his portrayal in art during the last 2,000 years.

K7.2   *Birthday Address.* New Haven: Yale Divinity School Visual Education Service. 1 sound cassette. (30 min). 1-7/8 ips. 4-track. Mono.

— Recorded on 29 March.

K7.3   "The Challenge of the Future (Part I)." In *Catalyst: A Resource for Christian Leaders* 6 (June): 6. 1 cassette. 2-track. "Catalyst Tape Talk" accompanies the cassette.

"The Challenge of the Future (Part 2): What Will Become of the Church?" In *Catalyst* 6 (July): 7. 1 cassette.

"The Challenge of the Future (Part 3): What Will become of Christianity?" In *Catalyst* 6 (August): 8. 1 cassette.

K7.4   Documentary Film of Roland H. Bainton. Made by Dale Lindquist, Yale School of Art. Information available from Yale Divinity School Visual Education Service.

K7.5   *Erasmus.* Columbus, Ohio: Evangelical Theological Seminary. 1 sound cassette analog. 1-7/8 ips.

— Chapel talk delivered in November.

K7.6   *Polish Women of the Reformation.* New Haven: Yale Divinity School Visual Education Service. 1 sound cassette (40 min). 1-7/8 ips. 4 track. Mono.

— Address about the role that women played in the Protestant Reformation in Poland.

1975

K8   *Women of the Reformation: Katherine von Bora, Katherine Zell, Charlotte de Bourbon.* Holden Village, Chelan, Washington: Holden Village Tape Ministry. 1 cassette. 2-track mono.

— Roland Bainton spoke about three women in *Women of the Reformation in Germany and Italy* (see A32) and *Women of the Reformation in France and England* (see A33).

1976

K9   *Erasmus and Luther: A Lecture and Sermon: Luther's Christmas Sermon.* Delivered by Roland H. Bainton at Eden Theological Seminary, 10 December. St. Louis: Eden Theological Seminary. 1 cassette tape. 2 1/2 " by 4". 1-7/8 ips.

1978

K9.1   *Chapel Address[es]*, 31 October–1 November. (Southern Baptist Theological Seminary). 2 sound cassettes. analog. Mono. 3 3/4 ips.

— "Jesus or Hamlet?" and "Bultmann and the Reformation."

— Julius Brown Gay Lectures, 1978–79.

— Recorded with chapel address by R. Michael Harton, 3 November.

K9.2   *The Church in the World.* Lutheran Hispanic Ministry. By Hilmer Krause. Minneapolis' Augsburg Publishing House. 1 sound cassette. analog. 1-7/8 ips.

— Includes RHB discussing Luther's use of New Testament materials.

— Resource: Series 5. No. 12. August.

K9.3   *Classroom Lecture[s].* 31 October–1 November. Southern Baptist Theological Seminary. 1 sound tape reel. analog. 3 3/4 ips. Mono. 7 in.

— "Conscience and the State," 31 October. Lecture delivered for the combined church history classes of Bill Leonard and Walter Shurden.

— "The History of Christian Art," 1 November. Classroom lecture for Glenn Hinson class.

— Recorded with chapel address, "Bultmann and the Reformation"

— "Just War Theory." 1 sound cassette. analog.

Talk given at Ethics Luncheon, 1 November.
All the above part of the Julius Brown Gay Lectures, 1978–79.

K9.35   [Erasmus and Luther: A Comparison]. Taped at San Francisco Theological Seminary, San Anselmo, Calif., 9 November 1978. 1 cassette. See O17.4.

K9.4   "Lecture on his book *Luther* and *Women of the Reformation*." Southern Baptist Theological Seminary. 1 video reel.

— Given during visit for Julius Brown Gay Lectures.

K9.5   *Luther and the Gospels*. (Louisville Presbyterian Theological Seminary). 1 sound cassette.

1979

K9.6   *Jesus Christ, God's Yes!* Minneapolis: Augsburg Publishing House, 1979. 1 sound cassette. analog. 1-7/8 ips.

— Several presentations including RHB's "Luther's Treatment of Biblical Discourse."

— Resource. Series 6, no. 5. January.

1981

K9.7   *History of the Christian Family*. New Haven: Yale Divinity School Visual Education Service. 1 sound cassette. 1-7/8 ips. 2 track. Mono.

— Listed in publisher's brochure as part of Family Forum Series.

— May have been issued first in the 1960s.

K9.8   *Impressions of a Trip to Poland*. New Haven: Yale Divinity School Visual Education Service. 2 sound cassettes.

K9.9   *Roland Bainton... Interviews.* New Haven: Yale Divinity School. 1 sound cassette. Interviewed by Parker Rossman.

K10   *Where Luther Walked* in video recording. Aid Association for Lutherans. Minneapolis, Minn.: Filmedia, Inc. and Worcester, Pa.: Gateway Films. Produced by Ray J. Christensen. Distributed by Vision Video. 1 videocassette. VHS. U standard. (39 min.).

        — Also issued as 16mm film, 1 film reel.

        — This film also available on the World Wide Web. Media Mart Video.<http://www.netvideo.com/mediamart/video/rel/sku/ mm10587.4html). See also U2.

        — Also issued in 1992 produced by Ray J. Christensen and Steve A. Kahenbeck (Charterhouse Learning Corporation). 1 videocassette. VHS. (30 min.).

K10.5   "Martin Luther's Christmas Sermon" in *Christmas.* Carol Stream, Ill.: Peaching Today, 1997. Preaching Today, 171. 1 sound cassette, analog, 1-7/8 ips. Mono

        — Recording also includes "The Foolishness of God" by Thomas K. Tewell, and "Design, Not Despair" by Gordon Terpstra.

Date Uncertain

K11   *Behold the Christ, Christian Views of Peace and War, and The Story of YDS.* Talks by RHB. New Haven: Yale Divinity School Visual Education Service. Cassette audiotapes.

        — Talks by RHB.

K12   *Women of the Reformation.* Written and narrated by RHB. 12" monaural record. 33 1/3 rpm.

        — RHB discusses four Reformation women.

WORKS
ABOUT
ROLAND H. BAINTON

L. BIBLIOGRAPHIES

1962

L1   Morris, Raymond P. "A Bibliography of Professor Bainton's Writings on the Reformation Period." In *Reformation Studies: Essays in Honor of Roland H. Bainton*,
edited by Franklin Hamlin Littell, 251–53. Richmond:
John Knox Press, 1962. See M1.

1964

Raymond P. Morris,
by RHB

L2   "Selected Bibliography of Roland H. Bainton." In *Collected Papers in
Church History, Series Three: Christian Unity and Religion in New England*,
283–89. Boston: Beacon Press, 1964. See A29.

— This bibliography ends with the year 1963. The same bibliography
appears in *Collected Papers II* (see A28) and through 1961 in *Collected
Papers I.* See A26.

— This bibliography is also included in the volume of *Archiv für
Reformationsgeschichte* dedicated to RHB in 1973. See also L5 and
O11.

— Roland H. Bainton Papers, Archives and Manuscripts, Yale Divinity School Library, holds the typescripts for this bibliography including
versions developed by Raymond P. Morris. Some include notes made
by RHB. See R1.

L3   Geisser, Heinrich, *Roland Bainton als Darsteller des 16. Jahrhunderts.* Semi-
nararbeit bei Herrn Prof. Dr. Werner Kaegi. Wintersemester 1968/9. 18
pages. Unpublished typescript. See also ND 1.

1972

L4   Dengler, Martha, *Roland Herbert Bainton: A Partial Bibliography.* Probably prepared for Dr. Patterson of the Pittsburgh School of Library Science. 27 March 1972. Unpublished typescript.

1973

L5   "Dedication: Selected Bibliography of Roland H. Bainton." In *Archiv für Reformationsgeschichte* 64 (1973): 5–12. See L2.

1974

L6   Dahl, Arlot. *Roland H. Bainton; A Bibliography.* 1974. 8 pages. Unpublished typescript.

L7   Morris, Raymond P. *Selected Reformation, Renaissance, Anabaptist, and Puritan Publications of Roland Herbert Bainton.* 4 pages. Typescript. Held by Yale Divinity School Archives, Archives and Manuscripts, Roland H. Bainton Papers.

M. FESTSCHRIFTEN

1962

M1   *Reformation Studies: Essays in Honor of Roland H. Bainton.* Edited by Franklin Hamlin Littell. Richmond: John Knox Press, 1962. 285 pages.

— Reviewed by the following:

Kent S. Knudson in *Religion in Life* 33:157–58.

Lewis W. Spitz in *Church History* 31 (1962): 463–64.

Cornelius Krahn in *Mennonite Quarterly Review* 38 (1964): 63–64.

C. J. Speel in *Journal of Bible and Religion* 31 (1963):256–57.

F. L. Battles in *Hartford Quarterly* 4 (1964): 85–88

Jacques Courvoisier in *Ecumenical Review* 16 (1964): 335–38.

Ernst-Wilhelm Kohls in *Archiv für Reformationsgeschichte* 56 (1965):120–22.

N. WORKS DEDICATED TO RHB

1958

N1   *Luther's World of Thought,* by Heinrich Bornkamm. Translated by Martin H. Bertram. St. Louis: Concordia Publishing House, 1958.

Heinrich Bornkamm
by RHB

1965

N2   *Renaissance Thought II: Papers on Humanism and the Arts,* by Paul Oskar Kristeller. New York: Harper and Row, 1965. Harper Torchbooks.

1967

N3   *Reconciliation and Renewal in Japan,* by Masao Takenaka. Revised edition. New York: Friendship Press, 1967.

1974

N4   *Studi Cinquecenteschi II: Aspetti della vita religiosa politica e letteraria,* by Benedetto Nicolini. Bologna: Tamari Editori, 1974.

NB. PUBLISHED BOOKS ABOUT AND WITH REFERENCE TO RHB

NB1   *Roland H. Bainton: An Examination of His Reformation Historiography*, by Steven H. Simpler, bibliography, 223–53. Lewiston, N.Y.: Edwin Mellen Press, 1985. 253 pages. (Texts and Studies in Religion, 24.)

      -Reviewed by:

      Eric W. Gritsch in *Church History* 56 (1987):272–73.

      James E. McGoldrick in *Fides and Historia* 19 (1987): 65–68.

      John Tonkin, "A Reformation Miscellany: Some Recent Books on Luther and the Reformation." In *Journal of Ecclesiastical History* 39 (July 1988): 445–54.

NB2   *The Radical Reformation*, by George Huntston Williams. 3d edition. Kirksville, Mo.: Sixteenth Century Journal Publishers, Inc., 1992.

      Reprinted Kirksville, Mo.: Truman State University Press, 2000. 1516 pp.

      — Reviewed in "Radicals and Radicalism: Historiography," in *Mennonite Quarterly Review* 67 (1993): 408–20.

      — E. E. Eminhizer, abstractor, says the following about this book, which discusses historical study of the sixteenth century from 1927 to 1990: "On the 30th anniversary of the publication of George H. Williams' *The Radical Reformation*, [this new edition] reviews the development of non-Lutheran scholarship on Anabaptist and other 'leftist' scholars such as Roland Bainton, William Pauck, Franklin H. Littell, and especially Harold S. Bender" (*ATLA Religion Database on CD-ROM*, 1996).

NB3   *The Reformation in Historical Thought*, by A. G. Dickens and John M. Tonkin with Kenneth Powell, 211, 223–24, 308, 350–51. Cambridge, Mass.: Harvard, 1985.

      — See introduction to this work, p. xv..

NB4   *Roly: Chronicles of a Stubborn Non-Conformist.* Edited by Ruth C. L. Gritsch. New Haven: Yale Divinity School, 1988. See A39.

      — Roland H. Bainton's autobiography.

O. ARTICLES ABOUT RHB

Reference Sources

Full documentation is not provided for all entries in this section. References by RHB in his papers were accepted as authoritative.

O1   *The Author's and Writer's Who's Who and Reference Guide*, 30. 1948–49.

       — 2d impression, 6th edition, 1971. (RHB's notes indicate he sent materials for 6th edition.)

       — 7th edition titled *World's Who's Who of Authors.*

O2   *Biographical Encyclopedia of the World*, 829. 1946.

O2.3   *The Blue Book: Leaders of the English Speaking World.* 1972 or later.

O2.5   *Cambridge Biographical Encyclopedia.*

O2.7   *Community Leaders of America.* 1974?

O2.9   *Contemporary Authors.* 29 January 1979.

O3   *Current Biography* 23 (June 1962): 6–8.

O4   *Current Biography Yearbook*, 20–23. 1962.

       — 1963.

O4.3   *Dictionary of International Biography*, vol. 9. 1973.

O4.5   *The Encyclopedia of the Lutheran Church.* 1965. Volume 2.

       — See article by Harold J. Grimm, "Luther Research."

O4.7   *International Authors and Writer's Who's Who*, 9th edition. 1981.

O4.9   *International Scholar's Directory*, 1st edition. March 1972.

O5   *International Who's Who* (1968–69): 71, (1972–73): 85, and (1974–75): 89.

O5.5   *International Who's Who in Arts and Antiquities* (sent September 1972).

O5.7   *The National Register of Prominent American and International Notables.*

O6   *Die Religion in Geschichte und Gegenwart.* Tübingen: Mohn, 1965. Registerband 7:10.

O6.5   *2000 Men of Achievement.* London: Marquis, 1969.

O7   *Who's Who in America* (1974–75): 74, (1975–76,):131, and (1978–79):143. (RHB references to v32, v37. 40th ed.)

O7.5   *Who's Who in the East.* 1969.

O8   *World Biography* (1948): 370–71, (1954): 56.

O9   *World's Who's Who of Authors.* 7th edition.

PERIODICAL SOURCES

O10   *Anchorage Daily News.* "Bainton Views Religion's Past, Future," by Jodi Stephens. Picture

O11   *Archiv für Reformationsgeschichte.* 64 (1973): 5–12. This volume is dedicated to RHB and includes a selective bibliography of his writings, significant biographical sketch, and a photograph. See also L2.

O11.9 [Billings, Montana newspaper].

"Dr. Bainton, retired Yale University ecclesiastical history professor, is visiting Billings on his way to Japan." Picture.

O12   *Bond* (October 1975): 3–4.

"Foremost Luther Scholar of Our Day: Meet Roland Bainton," by Herbert Brokering. Picture.

O12.3 *Boulder Sunday Camera.* 4 November 1979.

"Can Trust in Political System Be Restored: Non-Voter Erodes Democratic Process," by J. Edward Murray. Picture.

O13   *Christian Century* (9 April 1941): 97–98.

— "What Is Christianity?" by Charles Clayton Morrison. (Written record of an interview with Roland H. Bainton and others.)

O14   *Christian Thought* (June 1967): 86–95.

"Interview: Problems and Trends of the Modern Theological World," by Kenneth Scott Latourette, Roland H. Bainton, and Munug-hyuk Kim, 86–95. Picture on p. 87. (In Korean.)

O14.5 [Colfax, Washington newspaper]. 6 November 197?.

"Plymouth church marks 100th with worship, music, services."

— RHB, age 84, returned to his father's parish.

O14.6   [Dana College Alumni Publication]. (January 1980). "At 86, Bainton is Fascinating." See also O16.6.

— RHB gave four lectures at Dana College 12–16 January as "visiting theologian."

O14.7   *The Denver Post* (Friday, 28 March 1980): 38B.

"Church Historian Matches Broad Insight with Wit," by Virginia Culver, 38B (or 3BB). 2 pictures.

— Same article published in *Presbyterian Outlook*. See O22.5.

O15   *Drew Gateway.* (August 1952):15–17.

"Reformation History for the General Reader: Our Debt to Bainton," by J. S. Whale.

O15.5   *Encounter.* 26 (winter 1965): 87–96. "Recent Reformation Studies in Review," by Paul A. Crow.

O15.7   *Encounter.* 46 (autumn 1985): 339–56. "Luther, Luther Scholars, and the Jews," by Robert Michael.

— Also about Franklin Sherman, Martin Niemoller, Mark U. Edwards, and John Dobersteen.

O16   *Eschatology Today.* 4:1 (March 1978).

O16.2   *Fellowship.* November 1979. "Bainton Receives 1979 Gandhi Peace Award."

— Earlier recipients were Eleanor Roosevelt, Dorothy Day, Benjamin Spock, and Daniel Ellsberg.

O16.3   *Gospel Herald.* (19 October 1976): 802. "Roland Bainton: Church Historian," by Gregory I. Jackson.

O16.5   *Hartford Quarterly* 7 (summer 1967): 60–80. "Hooker: Puritanism: Democracy," by Robert S. Paul. See also D60.

— Also about Perry Miller, Thomas Hooker, church and state 1500–1599, New England Puritans, and covenant theology.,

O16.6   *The Hermes* (1980). Article by Sue Lazzaro.

— Student newspaper at Dana College. See O14.6.

O17   *Holden Village Courier* (spring 1978).

           — RHB is discussed throughout this 32-page issue. Picture on p. 14.

O17.3   *Ilkeston Advisor* (Friday, 20 June 1919).

           — From local newspaper of RHB's English birthplace in England not-
           ing the family's departure for Canada on the same day as the death of
           statesman William Gladstone.

           — Original clipping in Roland H. Bainton Papers at Yale Divinity
           School Library, Archives. See R1.

O17.4   *Independent-Journal.* San Rafael, California. (Friday, 17 November 1978)
           "Theologian: Ecumenism personal, meaningful," by Mary Leydecker.

           — Comments on RHB lectures given at San Francisco Theological
           Seminary, a Presbyterian institution in San Anselmo, and Golden Gate
           Baptist Theological Seminary.

O17.5   *International Journal of Religious Education.* 41 (April 1965). "The Greatest
           Single Force," by Virgil E. Foster. See also P18.

O18   *Journal of Presbyterian History* 51 (fall 1973):251–66. "Churchmen à la
           Roland H. Bainton," edited by J. H. Smylie.

O19   *The Lutheran* (4 February 1981).

           — Article includes RHB, with picture, on the subject of cablecasts.
           Discusses "Lutherans in Person" series for cable TV.

O20   *Materialdienst des Konfessionskundlichen Instituts.* 6 (1955):15–16. "Roland
           Bainton zum Martin Luther Film," by Gerhard Beetz.

O20.3   *The Milford Citizen.* (Sunday, 14 October 1979). "City Peace Foundation
           Makes Gandhi Award."

O20.5   *Mennonite Quarterly Review* 59 (October 1985): 350–61. "David Joris: A
           Prolegomenon to Further Research," by James M. Stayer.

           — Also concerns research of David and Nikolaas Berdijk, Friedrich
           Nipple, Klaus Deppermann, and S. Zijlstra.

O20.6   *Mennonite Quarterly Review* 61 (1987): 347–62. "Anabaptist Women of
           the North: Peers in the Faith, Subordinates in Marriage," by M. Lucille
           Marr.

— Also discusses views of George H. Williams, Thomas F. Safley, and Joyce L. Irwin.

O20.7 *Mirror.* Augustana College [Sioux Falls, South Dakota] 65 (22 October 1981). "Reformation Events Highlight Weekend."

— Notes RHB's participation in 23–25 October Festival of Renaissance and Reformation and the Staley Distinguished Christian Scholar Series.

O20.9 [Naugatuck, Connecticut newspaper]. (12–13 April 1980). "Reknowned Historian Lecture Series Speaker."

— Announces RHB speaking for the Fred W. Moeckel, Jr. Memorial Lecture Series at Hillside Covenant Church in Naugatuck. Topics included "The Church, the World, and Survival," "Luther's Treatment of Scripture," and "Jesus or Hamlet."

O21 *New Haven Register.*

"Abingdon-Cokesbury Award to Roland H. Bainton." (4 June 1950): sec. 7, p. 8.

"Alcohol Study Class to Open at Yale July 7." (May 16, 1946).

— Annouces RHB as lecturer.

"Bainton Wins $7,500 Award for Biography: Manuscript on Martin Luther by Yale Educator Adjudged Best" (21 September 1949).

"Bainton Will Receive Gandhi Peace Award," by John Knoble. (fall 1979):12. Picture.

"Faces and Facts," by Willis Birchman. (Sunday, 25 April 1943).

"For Catholics and Protestants: Recommended Lenten Season Reading Picked by Mrs. Luce, Professor Bainton" (1 March 1953). Picture.

"He's Being Honored" (February 1974).

"Lenten Preacher" (22 March 1950). Picture.

"Man of Many Faces," by John Knoble. (28 February 1971):20–23.

"Peace Honor Brings Hope of Progress," by John Knoble. (24 October 1979). Sunday pictorial section.

O21   *New Haven Register* (Continued).

— Article by former student of RHB who had known him for thirty-one years. Report on Promoting Enduring Peace organization's Gandhi Peace Award.

"Professor Bainton, Cyclist 28 Years, Has Covered 112,000 Rugged Miles" (8 February 1948): sec. 1, p. 20. Picture and RHB caricature of himself.

"Professor Tells Story in Cinema," by John Knoble. (18 October 1981). Metro-Forum Section.

— Describes RHB's contributions at age 87 to film "Where Luther Walked." See K9.5.

"Rev. R.H. Bainton, Bike-Riding Author, Caricaturist, Retiring from Yale's Divinity School after 42 Years" (1 July 1962):12. Picture.

— Roland H. Bainton Papers, Yale Divinity School Archives, also includes Yale University News Bureau release to newspapers Sunday, 1 July 1962. Six-page typescript.

"Roland Bainton: The Intellect Never Rests," by Bill Lazarus. (Thursday, 15 December 1983), Living Section, p. 70. Three pictures.

— Reports on RHB's last speech, taped and sent to St. Matthew's Lutheran Church, White Plains, New York when RHB was age 90.

"Trio Finds Soviet Domination Hasn't Broken Polish Spirit," by John Knoble. (25 May 1975): sec. A, p.10.

"Yale Educator Gets Honor Degree from Germany after 2-year Delay" (17 March 1950). Picture.

"Yule Release of Reds asked by Petitioners."

— Notes that RHB as well as Mrs. Roosevelt were in group asking for leniency for Communists.

O22   *New York Times.*

"Abingdon-Cokesbury Award to Roland H. Bainton" (4 June 1950): sec. 7, p. 8.

"Christmas: A Sermon by Luther," by Kenneth A. Briggs. (Thursday, 16 December 1983)

— Describes RHB's traditional Christmas presentation. This presentation was his final one given at the age of 88. (RHB died in 1984.)

"1500 Christian Clergy Sign Open Letter to Truman which Dr. Heuss Refused to Sign" (14 January 1953):19.

— Concerns Rosenberg clemency appeal.

"46 Urge Christmas Amnesty for 16 Communists Imprisoned under Smith Act of 1940; Delay for 180 Cases Now Awaiting Trial or Outcome of Appeals; Appeal to Eisenhower " (21 December 1955):20.

"Harvard Alumni Elect: Rev. D. McL. Greeley Chosen to Head Divinity Group" (27 April 1955).

"Letter by 12 U.S. Clergymen and Educators Urges Repentance [for bombing Hiroshima]; Condemns Bomb Use" (3 August 1955):22.

"Sermon on Christianity and the World" (9 August 1937):17.

"Sermon on Love of God" (8 July 1940):20.

"Sermon on Peace" (11 July 1935):17.

"Yale Teacher, 79, Rides Bike and Keeps Campus Enthralled" (Sunday, 24 February 1974).

"Yale University: Professor Bainton Retires" (1 July 1962): 47.

O22.5   *Presbyterian Outlook* (5 May 1980). "The Wit and Wisdom of Roland Bainton," by Virginia Culver. From Religious News Service.

O23   *Publisher's Weekly* 156 (8 October 1949):1665. "Abingdon-Cokesbury Award."

O24   *Reflection* [Yale Divinity School].

"Bainton Portrait Unveiled" 72 (November 1974): 3.

"From the Quad" 71 (May 1974): 4. "Roland Bainton's Birthday... Gift for Portrait Announced." Picture.

"From the Quad" 72 (May 1975): 3. "Bainton Portrait."

— Issue has image of the portrait of RHB as cover.

O24   *Reflection* [Yale Divinity School] (continued).

"From the Quad" 78 (November 1980). "Opening Convocation" [Service in Remembrance of Luther Weigle on 4 September, 100th Anniversary of his birthday].

— Includes mention of RHB's statement.

"Making the Roland Bainton Documentary" 7 (January 1974):10–11.

O24.5   *Reflections*

"Vintage Bainton: On the Occasion of the Centenary of His Birth" (winter/spring 1994):15–17. Picture.

— Comments on RHB's "straightforward speech."

— Reprint from *Yale Divinity School News* (May 1938):1–3.

O25   *Sixteenth Century Journal* 14 (spring 1983): 3–11. "*Humanitas Pietas*: The Shoulders on Which We Stand," by Miriam Usher Chrisman.

— Address delivered to Sixteenth Century Studies Conference, St. Louis, Missouri. (30 October 1982). Appreciation expressed for RHB and Harold Grimm.

O26   [Statesboro, Georgia newspaper] (1973). "Georgia Southern to Hear Historian." Picture.

O27   *Sun-Times* [Chicago]. "Preposterous Nativity and Such a Cradle," by Roy Larson. Picture.

O28   *Time* 80 (13 July 1962): 42. "Lost Leaders."

O29   *Yale Alumni Magazine.*

"Bicyclist Bainton," by C. Howard Hopkins. [Letter to the Editor] (December 1974):2, 4.

"The Bicycling Professor. " [Letters to the Editor] (December 1976):2–3.

"Professors Emeriti." Photographs by Phyllis Crowley. ("Roland Bainton: Titus Street Professor of Ecclesiastical History," photograph and statement by RHB.) (October 1977):14.

"Profile: Roland Bainton," by Lynn Horsley (13 April 1982):29. Picture and two self-caricatures by RHB.

O29.5   *Yale Daily News.*

"Here he rides: a portrait of Roland Bainton," by John Nassikes (Monday, 12 February 1979): 3 and 6.

O30   *Yale Divinity School.* The Great Yale Tradition. "A Word from Roland Bainton," with reproduction of the Deane Keller portrait (September 1975):26–27.

O31   *Yale Divinity School: A Special Issue of the Yale Divinity News* 58 (May 1961):10.

O32   *Yale Divinity News* (1917–).

References to RHB appear in numerous issues. His lectures, publications, activities, and sketches were part of the news of the Yale Divinity School community until his death in 1984.

O32.5   *Yale Historical Bulletin* 20 (1962):14. [RHB] by George Pierson. Self-caricature by RHB.

O32.7   *Yale University News Bureau. Faculty Information Service.*

"Biography of the Reverend Roland H. Bainton." (December 1976). 3-page typescript. Roland H. Bainton Papers. See R1.

O32.8   *Yale University News Release* (Yale University News Bureau). "For Release to Sunday papers" (17 February 1974). 6 pages.

— Announcement of convocation in honor of RHB at Yale Divinity School.

O33   *Yale Weekly Bulletin and Calendar.*

— Announcement of convocation honoring RHB held 19–20 February 1974 (18–25 February 1974):1.

— References to RHB occur throughout the *Bulletin* from 1917–1985.

REFERENCES TO RHB IN BOOKS

O34   *Bible Words that Guide Me*, edited by Hubert A. Elliot, 11–13. New York: Grosset and Dunlop, 1963.

O35   *For Peace and Justice: Pacifism in America, 1914–1941*, by Charles Chatfield, 51–52. Knoxville: University of Tennessee Press, 1971.

— Mentioned by Simpler in his book. See NB1.

O36   *Living in Today's World*, edited by Masao Takenaka. n.d.

— Published for an occasion of the Nippon Christian Academy, Kansai Seminar House, Kyoto, Japan. Picture of RHB.

O37   "Roland H. Bainton: A Biographical Appreciation," by Georgia Harkness. In *Reformation Studies: Essays in Honor of Roland H. Bainton*, edited by Franklin Hamlin Littell, 11–18. Richmond: John Knox Press, 1963.

O38   *Waiilatpu*. Whitman College Yearbook, 7:7–8, 132, 135. Kenosha, Wis.: George Banta Publishing Co. for Collegiate Press, 1913.

— RHB's caricatures and sculpture are also noted in this volume. See J24.

— May also be included in volumes for 1910–12 and 1914.

OB. OBITUARIES AND *IN MEMORIA*

OB1   Chrisman, Miriam Usher. "In Memoriam." *Archiv für Reformationsgeschichte* 76 (1985): 5.

— Obituary for RHB (d. 1984) and Harold J. Grimm (d.1983).

OB2   Gritsch, Eric W. "In Memoriam Roland H. Bainton, 1894–1984." *Lutheran Theological Seminary Bulletin* 68 (winter 1985): 62–63.

— "Martin Luther Colloquium, 1984: Luther, Humanism, and the Educated Pastor." Lutheran Theological Seminary, Gettysburg, Pa. O31: Papers.

OB3   Hendrix, S. "In Memoriam Roland H. Bainton." In *Lutherjahrbuch 1985: Organ der internationalen Luther-forschung,* 9–12. (Göttingen: Vandenhoech und Ruprecht, 1985). (Lutherjahrbuch, 52.)

— 8th International Congress for Luther Research.

— Bibliography, 303–96.

OB4   Keck, Leander. "In Memory of Roland Bainton, 1894–1984." *Reflection* 82 (November 1984): 5. Picture.

— From Memorial Service at Yale Divinity School.

— Comments also by Raymond Morris and Davie Napier. Prayer by John Vannorsdal Raymond: 6–7. Pictures.

OB5   Kingdon, Robert M. "In Memoriam: Roland H. Bainton." *Sixteenth Century Journal* 15 (spring 1984):105–106.

— Obituary with picture.

OB6   "Bainton, Roland H." *Current Biography* 45 (June 1984): 45,47 (1).

OB7   Associated Press obituary, 13 February 1984.

OM. BAINTON BOOK PRIZE

OM1   The Roland H. Bainton Book Prize is awarded annually in honor of Bainton by the Sixteenth Century Studies Conference. In 1996, the Prize was expanded to three categories: theology and history, literature, and art and music. Recipients of the award through 1999 are listed below. Winners are announced each October at the Conference and in a subsequent issue of *The Sixteenth Century Journal*. The criteria for the prize may be found at http://www2.truman.edu/escj/scsc/prizes/bainton.html.

1990   William Kerrigan and Gordon Braden, *The Idea of the Renaissance*. Johns Hopkins Press.

1991   Timothy Hampton, *Writing from History: The Rhetoric of Exemplarity in Renaissance Literature*. Cornell University Press.

1992   Tessa Watt, *Cheap Print and Popular Piety, 1550–1640*. Cambridge University Press.

1993   Lisa Jardine, *Erasmus, Man of Letters: Construction of Charisma in Print*. Princeton University Press.

1994   Sara Nalle, *God in La Mancha: Religious Reform and the People of Cuenca 1500–1650*. Johns Hopkins University Press.

1995   Erik H. C. Midelfort, *The Mad Princes of Renaissance Germany*. University Press of Virginia.

1996   Benjamin J. Kaplan, *Libertines and Calvinists: Confession and Community in Utrecht, 1578–1620*. Oxford University Press.
Martha Feldman, *City Culture and the Madrigal in Venice*, University of California Press.
Katherine Eisaman Maus, *Inwardness and the Theater in the English Renaissance*. University of Chicago Press.

1997   Michael Graham, *The Uses of Reform: 'Godly Discipline' and Popular Behavior in Scotland and Beyond, 1560-1610*. E.J. Brill.
James Shapiro, *Shakespeare and the Jews*. Cambridge University Press

Carolyn C. Wilson , *Italian Paintings, XIV-XVI Centuries, in the Museum of Fine Arts, Houston*. Museum of Fine Arts, Houston.

1998   Susan Karant-Nunn, *The Reformation of Ritual: An Interpretation of Early Modern Germany.* Routledge
Anthony Grafton, *The Footnote: A Curious History.* Harvard University Press
Hans J. Hillerbrand, editor, *Oxford Encyclopedia of the Reformation,* 4 vols. Oxford University Press.

1999   Jeffrey Hamburger, *The Visual and the Visionary: Art and Female Spirituality in Late Medieval German.* Zone Books.
Lorraine Daston and Katharine Park, *Wonders and the Order of Nature, 1150–1750.* Zone Books.
Peter Godman, *From Polizano to Machiavelli: Florentine Humanism in the High Renaissance.* Princeton University Press

P. REVIEWS OF RHB'S MONOGRAPHS

Reviews of Roland Bainton's books have appeared in many scholarly journals, popular magazines, and countless newspapers in many countries. To locate all of them would be an impossible task. Included here are many of them gathered from Bainton's own files, from published index citations, and from perusal of those journals to which Roland Bainton regularly contributed. A number of items from varied sources have been omitted because of uncertain bibliographical information. Hopefully what remains will offer a selection of review materials helpful in discerning how RHB's works were received by his various readers.

P1   *Behold the Christ* (1974). See A34.
America 131:262–63. Virginia McNally.
Chicago Theological Seminary Register 64:55–56.
Choice 11:1762.
Christian Century 91:728.
Christian Scholar's Review 7261–63. Elizabeth A. Douglas.
The Disciple 2:30. James Stayer.
Foundations (Baptist) 19:380–81.
Library Journal 99:1931. Felix L. Hirsch.
The Living Church 169:18. Eleanor S. Wainwright.
Lutheran Libraries 17:42. Barbara Ann Wengert.
Lutheran Quarterly 26:469–70. Eric H. Wahlstrom.
Music Ministry 7:38–39.
New Book Review (May 1974): 9.
Perkins School of Theology Journal 28:45–46. Victor P. Furnish.
Presbyterian Outlook 156:15. Roland Mushat Frye.

P1   *Behold the Christ* (1974) (Continued).
       Religious Education 70:344–45. John W. Dixon, Jr.
       Times Literary Supplement (3 January 1975):20. P. Hebblethwaite.

P2   *Bernardino Ochino* (1941). See A6.
       American Historical Review 47:580–82. Frederic C. Church.
       Church History 11:254. Lamberto Borghi.
       Il Libro Italiano (Rome) 2:1938.
       Nuova Rivista Storica (Milan) 25:168. F. Bolgiani.
       Rinascita (Florence) 5:213–20. P. Cherubelli.

P3   *Bibliography of the Continental Reformation* (1935). See A3.
       Bibliographical Society of America. Papers 68:96.
       Church History 4:243. Wilhelm Pauck.
       Historische Zeitschrift 152:638.
       Revue d'Histoire Ecclésiastique 31:872. A. de Meyer.
       Sixteenth Century Journal 4:121–21. Robert Kolb.
       Zeitschrift für Kirchengeschichte 55:707–708. E. Wolf.

P4   *Bibliography of the Continental Reformation* (1972). See A3.
       Choice 10:751.
       Church History 43:542–43. Maria Grossman.
       Churchman 87:148–49. G. E. Duffield.
       Review for Religious 32:943. C. Whiteman.
       Sixteenth Century Journal 4:121–22. Robert Kolb.

P5   *Christendom* (1966). See A30.
       Choice (reviews vol. 1) 4:301.
       Christian Century (vol. 1) 8:1057; (vol. 2) 84:1576.

P6   *Christian Attitudes toward War and Peace* (1960). See A22.
       Adult Teacher (August 1961):14. F. H. Schisler.
       Baptist Leader 28:72. E. T. O.
       Brethren Life and Thought 6:60. Edward Krusen Zeigler.
       Canadian Baptist 107:12. W. F. S.
       Catholic Historical Review 50:73. H. Koenig.
       Christian Century 78:115. Allen Hackett.
       The Churchman (St. Petersburg) 175:13. Gardiner M. Day.
       Concern 3:6. H. Will, Jr.
       Current Thought on Peace and War 2:19–20.
       Encounter 22:358–59. John M. Swomley, Jr.
       Fellowship 22:358–59. Kenneth Scott Latourette.

Free Methodist 94:126. J. Paul Taylor.
Friends Journal 7:35. Joseph R. Kaisner.
Friends Journal 12:423. R. R. W.
Gettysburg Seminary Bulletin (May 1962). Eric Gritsch.
Indian Journal of Theology 12:37–39. Vinay C. Samuel.
Japan Christian Quarterly 29:61–62. C. H. Powles.
Journal of Bible and Religion 30:237–41. C. B. Joynt.
Journal of Church and State 3:93–94. Olin T. Binkley.
Kirkus 28:898.
Library Journal 85:2940.
Lutheran Quarterly 13:184–85. D. A. Lund.
Mennonite Life 16:143. Esko Loewen.
Mennonite Quarterly Review 35:322–24. Guy F. Hershberger.
Motive 21:45.
Perkins School of Theology Journal 15:52–53. Franklin H. Littell.
Quaker History 51:1962. F. B. T.
Religion in Life 31:134–35. T. R. Weber
Review and Expositer 58:394. Henlee H. Barnette.
Review of Religious Research 3:42–43. Kenneth
    Scott Latourette.
Saints Herald 7:15. John W. Bradley.
Signs of the Times of the Yale Divinity School
    1:11–12. Richard Marius.
Theology Today 19:133–37. J. Lawrence
    Burkholder.

Kenneth Scott Latourette,
by RHB

Union Seminary Quarterly Review 16:339–41.
    John C. Bennett.
Westminster Bookman 20:18–19. Roger L. Shinn.
Workers with Youth 15:18.

P7   *The Church of Our Fathers* (1941). See A7.
    American Historical Review 47:175–76. William Wilson Manross.
    Anglican Theological Review 24:173. Jean H. Johnson.
    Booklist 37:444
    Christendom 6:3. James Clarke.
    Christian Century 58:499. W. E. Garrison.
    Christian Century 88:1092.
    Christian Century 88:1386.
    Church History 10:378. Ross Snyder.
    The Churchman 155:19. Robert C. Batchelder.

P7   *The Church of Our Fathers* (1941) (Continued).
      Counsel 2:4–6.
      Crozer Quarterly 18:350. R. E. E. Harkness.
      Expository Times 59:263.
      Harvard Educational Review October, 1941:508–509. William E.
         Vickery.
      Holy Cross Magazine 52:184. Karl Tiedemann.
      Horn Book Magazine 17:294. Ben Roberts.
      International Journal of Religious Education 17:38. Herman J. Sweet.
      Japan Christian Quarterly 20:74. Philip Williams.
      Journal of Bible and Religion 9:254. Edna M. Baxter.
      Library Journal 66:619. Eleanor Kidder.
      Lutheran School Journal 77:45. E. H. E.
      New York Herald Tribune Books (20 December 1953): 9. Louise S.
         Bechtel.
      New York Times Book Review (13 April 1941):12.
      Revista Liturgica Argentine 218:76–77.
      Revue d'Histoire et de Philosophie Religieuse 46:182. B. Roussel.
      Theology 51:351–52. Ruth Rouse.
      Wisconsin Library Bulletin 37:205.
      Yale Divinity News (March 1941): 4–7. J. C. S.

P8   *Collected Papers in Church History, Series I–III* (1962–64). See A26, 28, 29.
      Archiv für Reformationsgeschichte 56:112–13. Ernst-Wilhelm Kohls.

P9   *Collected Papers in Church History, Series I: Early and Medieval Christianity*
      (1962). See A26.
      Archiv für Reformationsgeschichte 56:112–13.
      American Historical Review 8:1801. Harold J. Grimm.
      Bangor Alumni Bulletin 38:4. Charles S. Partridge.
      Catholic Historical Review 49:396–98. John Kemp.
      Chicago Theological Seminary Register 53:50–51. John T. McNeill.
      Christian Advocate 6:18. Richard M. Cameron.
      Christian Century 79:1068.
      Church History 31:457–58. Frederick A. Norwood.
      Colgate Rochester Bulletin 35:B. Charles Merritt Nielsen.
      Iliff Review 19:43. H. Gordon Van Sickle.
      Journal of Bible and Religion 30:328–32. Charles J. Speel.
      Journal of Ecclesiastical History 14:216–17. S. L. Greenslade.
      Journal of Religion 43:160. John Opie.

Library Journal 87:2382. J. A. Clarke.
The Living Church 145:2–3. L. G. Patterson.
Lutheran Quarterly 16:83. R. E. Hanson.
Review of Metaphysics (December 1962): 392. R. C. N.
Speculum 38:107.
Union Seminary Quarterly Review 18:65–69. Virgil R. Westlund.
Unitarian Universalist Register-Leader 143:19.

P10   *Collected Papers in Church History, Series II: Studies on the Reformation*
(1963). See A28.
American Ecclesiastical Review 150:449. B. Barthaler.
Archiv für Reformationsgeschichte 54:112–13. Ernst-Wilhelm Kohls.
Catholic Historical Review 50:567. H. Müller.
Christian Advocate 8:17. F. H. Littell.
Christian Century 81:365.
Church History 33:101–102. Brian A. Gerrish.
Church History 50:567. H. Müller.
Ecumenical Review 16:579–81. A. D. Lewis.
Iliff Review 21:48–49. H. Gordon Van Sickle.
International Journal of Religious Education, 41. Gerald E. Knoff.
Journal of Religion 46:83–84. John Opie.
Lutheran Quarterly 16:83–84. Bernhard Erling.
Odrodzenie i Reformacja w Polsce 10:266. Lech Szczucki.
Religion in Life 33:485. Charles Garside.
Scottish Journal of Theology 19:245–46. J. Atkinson.
Southwestern Journal of Theology 6:142. W. R. Estep.
Theological Studies 25:482. R. McNally.
Times Literary Supplement (23 December 1965):1201.
Union Seminary Quarterly Review 19:168–69. J. B. Thomas.
Westminster Bookman 23:1.
Yale Review 53:viii.

P11   *Collected Papers in Church History, Series III: Christian Unity and Religion in
New England* (1964). See A29.
Archives de Sociologie des Religions 11:160–61. Jean Séguy.
Church History 34:219–20. Emil Oberholzer.
Colgate-Rochester Bulletin 37:3. Winthrop S. Hudson.
Dialog 4:235–36. Harris E. Kassa.
Expository Times 77:125–26. Johnston R.McKay.
Journal for the Scientific Study of Religion 4:270-2. Martin E. Marty.

P11   *Collected Papers in Church History, Series III* (Continued)
       Library Journal 89:1759.
       Lutheran Quarterly 16:374. Frederick K. Wentz.
       Princeton Seminary Bulletin 58:57. James Hastings Nichols.
       Religion in Life 34:159. J. D. Lee.
       Times Literary Supplement (2 December 1965):1111.
       Union Seminary Quarterly Review 21:63–65. Albert Rabil, Jr.

P12   *Concerning Heretics* (1935). See A4.
       Anglican Theological Review A18:49–50. P. V. Norwood.
       Archiv für Reformationsgeschichte 41:173–74. Walter Köhler.
       Catholic Historical Review 22:445–47. Francis J. Tschan.
       Christian Century 53:1616. John T. McNeill.
       Church History 5:100–102. Wilhelm Pauck.
       Commonweal 23:56.
       Crozer Quarterly 13:153.
       English Historical Review 52:1360. E. W. W.
       London Quarterly and Holborn Review (April 1936):176–77.
       Mid-America 7:71. Joseph Roubik.
       Theologische Literaturzeitung 63:32. Walter Köhler.
       Times Literary Supplement (14 March 1936):215.
       Yale Divinity News (November 1935): 43. R. L. C.
       Zeitschrift für Kirchengeschichte 55:409–11. Elizabeth Feist.

P13   *David Joris* (1937). A5.
       American Historical Review 43:695. Preserved Smith.
       Archiv für Reformationsgeschichte 34:138–39. H. Volz.
       Bulletin de la Société de l'Histoire du Protestantisme Française 86:391–92.
       Christliche Welt 52:240. Otto Clemen.
       Church History 7:280. Harold S. Bender.
       Historische Zeitschrift 159:116–29. K. Bauer.
       Journal of Modern History 10:297–98. Charles Lyttle.
       Kirchenblatt für die Reformierte Schweiz 11:173. Rudolf Schwarz.
       Mennonitische Geschichte Blätter 3:94. Cornelius Krahn.
       Studi Germanici 2:323–24. Delio Cantimori.
       Theologie der Gegenwart 32:26–27. E. Wolf.
       Theologische Literaturzeitung 63:257.

P14   *Early Christianity* (1960). See A23.
       Christian Advocate 5:23.
       Greek Orthodox Theological Review 7:168–69. John E. Rexine.

P15   *Erasmus of Christendom* (1969). See A31.
       America 121:534. Maurice Adelman.
       American Historical Review 77:128–29. James D. Tracy.
       Andover Newton Quarterly 11:48–49. J. Earl Thompson, Jr.
       Andrews University Seminary Studies 9:68–69. Viggo Olsen.
       Anglican Digest (autumn 1969):22.
       Basler Nachrichten 297:25.
       Book Newsletter of Augsburg Publishing House 413:4.
       Booklist 65:1138.
       British Weekly (28 May 1970): 4. E. H. Robertson.
       Bulletin of the Congregational Library 20:3. John A. Harrer.
       Calvin Theological Journal 5:87–88. John Kromminga.
       Canadian Journal of History / Annales Canadiennes d'Histoire 5:98–100.
          J. McConica.
       Catholic Historical Review 57:512. G. Marc'hadour.
       Choice 6:998.
       Christ in der Gegenwart 23:294.
       Christian Century 86:996. Philip S. Watson.
       Church History 41:524–27. Clyde L. Manschreck.
       Church History Review 57:512–15. G. Marc'hadour.
       Church Management (July 1969): 51. William L. Ludlow.
       Church Quarterly 3:253–54. Gordon Rupp.
       Cross and Crown 2:108. R. Weber.
       Cross Currents 20:97–98. Donald Nugent.
       Dansk Teologisk Tidskrift 35:229. J. L. Bailley.
       Dialog 9:155–56. Michael Blecker.
       European Studies Review 1:75–77. Margaret Mann Philips.
       Evangelical Quarterly 43:47–48. Timothy C. F. Stunt.
       Expository Times 82:97–98. Timothy C. F. Stunt.
       Friends Journal (15 February 1970):105. Stephen Sebert.
       Geschichte im Wissenschaft und Unterricht 26:651–62.
       Heythrop Journal 12:150–63. M. A. Screech.
       The Historian 32:473–74. Gordon Griffiths.
       Historische Zeitschrift 1:127–28. August Baek.
       Iliff Review 29:48–52.
       Irenikon 45:437.
       Journal of Church and State 13:150–51. Robert C. Walton.
       Journal of Modern History 44:249–51. Peter G. Bietenholz.
       Journal of Religion 50:207–208. John Howie.

P15   *Erasmus of Christendom* (1969) (Continued).
Journal of the American Academy of Religion 39:100–102, 104. Albert
Rabil, Jr.
Kirchenblatt für die Reformierte Schweiz 13:74.
Kirkus 36:22. John L. Castael and J. F. Bernard.
Library Journal 94:184. Felix E. Hirsch.
Literature Survey: A Review of Recent Theological Publications 4:380–83.
Lewis W. Spitz.
Liturgical Arts 38:29. A. Godfrey.
Lutheran Forum (October 1969): 32–33. Lewis W. Spitz.
Lutheran World 16:380–83. Lewis W. Spitz.
Modern Language Review 68:649. F. M. Higman.
The Month 2:90. Donald Nugent.
Münchener Theologische Zeitschrift 24:179–80. Hermann Tüchle.
Nederlands Archief voor Kerkgeschiedenis 53:143–44. D. de B.
New Blackfriars 54:96. C. Allmand.
New Leader 52:19–20. Edouard Roditi.
New York Times Book Review (4 May 1969):14, 16. Charles W.
Ferguson.
Princeton Seminary Bulletin 62:101–102. N. V. Hope.
Recherches de Science Religieuse 61:294–96. Joseph Lecler.
Referatedienst zur Literaturwissenschaft 1:51–52. Heinz Eritner.
Erasmus of Christendom .
Reformierte Kierchenzeitung: Theologische Literaturbeiträge 113:16. K. H.
Religion and Society 16:43–46. Robert Thornton.
Religion in Life 38:470–71. Wilhelm Pauck.
Religious Studies Bulletin 3:166–67.
Recherches de Science Religieuse 61:294–6. Joseph Lecler.
Referatedienst zur Literaturwissenschaft 1:51–52. Heinz Eritner.
Reformierte Kirchenzeitung: Theologische Literaturbeiträge 113:16. K. H.
Religion and Society 16:43–46. Robert Thornton.
Religion in Life 38:470–71. Wilhelm Pauck.
Religious Studies Bulletin 3:166–67.
Review and Expositor (October 1969): 445–46. Glenn Hinson.
Review for Religious 28:850. John P. Donnelly.
Revue d'Histoire Ecclésiastique 68:832–33. Georges Chantraine.
Revue d'Histoire et de Philosophie Religieuse 67:101–102.
Scottish Journal of Theology 24:369–71. Basil Hall.
Scripture Bulletin 3:47. J. McGurk.

South Atlantic Quarterly 69:409. A. B. Ferguson.
Spectator 224:713. G. D. Ramsey.
Theologische Literaturzeitung 99:520–21. Ingetraut Ludolphy.
Theologische Revue 65:446.
Thought 45:155. J. C. Olin.
Time (25 April 1969): 69–70.
Times Literary Supplement (29 April 1970): 483.
Union Seminary Quarterly Review 25:243–46. David W. Lotz.
Western Humanities Review 24:93. E. M. Huenemann.
Westminster Theological Journal. 33:1056. A. D. MacLeod.
Yale Review 59:278–81. Thomas M. Greene.

P16   *George Lincoln Burr* (1943). See A28.
American Historical Review 49:75–76. Gertrude Randolph Bramlette
    Richards.
Catholic Historical Review 30:61–63.
Church History 12:297–99. Charles H. Lyttle.
English Historical Review 59:286–87. G. P. G.
Journal of American History 30:600.
Medium Aevum 13:22–26. F. M. Powicke.
New York Times (1 August 1943): sec. 7:19. Julian P. Boyd.

P17   *Here I Stand* (1950). See A11.
American Historical Review 56:863–66. G. C. Sellery.
American Lutheran 33:18–20. Adolf F. Meyer.
American Lutheran 34:6–8, 29–30. Richard Klann.
Archiv für Kulturgeschichte 36:394–95. Robert Stupperich.
Archiv für Reformationsgeschichte 42:265–66. D.
    Hermann Dörries.
Book Newsletter of Augsburg Publishing House 119:2–
    3. E. Clifford Nelson.
British Weekly (3 April 1952): 8–11. John Hus
    (humorous issue).
Calvin Forum 16:193. Albert Hyma.
Catholic Historical Review 37:302–304. Herbert J.
    Clancy.

Hermann Dörries,
by RHB

Catholic World 172:398. F. D. Cohalan.
The Chaplain (January/February 1951): 37. Robert J. Plumb.
Chicago Sunday Tribune (1 October 1950): 6. L. T. Heron.
Christian Century 67:1168–69. Donald J. Campbell.

P17   *Here I Stand* (1950) (Continued).

Christian Century 67:1169. W. E. Garrison.

Christian Century 72:335. Theodore A. Gill.

Christian Register 130:7. Duncan Howlett.

Christian Science Monitor (28 October 1950): 6. Neil Martin.

Church History 20:73–74. Harold J. Grimm.

Classmate (Methodist). 70:23.

Crozer Quarterly 28:362. R. J. Bean.

Deutsche Literaturzeitung 74:540–41. Martin Doerne.

Evangelisch-Lutherische Kirchenzeitung 5:82–83. Hans Preus.

Expository Times (April 1951):101–102. W. S. Urquaut.

Freies Christentum 4:88–89. Hermann Werdermann.

Harvard Divinity School Bulletin 15:69–70.

Hibbert Journal (April 1952): 311–12. Roger Thomas.

Historische Zeitschrift 173:132–33. Heinrich Bornkamm.

International Journal of Religious Education 27:32. Harry H. Kolas.

Journal of Bible and Religion 19:81–82. Winthrop S. Hudson.

Journal of Modern History 24:190–91. Garrett Mattingly.

Journal of Pastoral Care 4:55. Don C. Shaw.

Kirkus 18:590.

Lutheran Quarterly 3:224–25. R. Roth.

Der Lutheraner 6:368. H. W. Huebner.

Mennonite Life 6:47. Cornelius Krahn.

Nation 171:350.

New Haven Register (12 November 1950): 8. W. H. Veale.

Cornelius Krahn,
by RHB

New York Times Book Review (19 November 1950):10. Thomas Caldecott Chubb.

Past and Present 2:60.

Presbyterian Outlook 132:43. Ernest Trice Thompson.

Pulpit Digest (October 1956): 93. Robert E. Luccock.

Renaissance News 4:30:2. Harold J. Grimm.

Revue des Sciences Religieuses (April 1953):152–55.

Saturday Review of Literature 34:37. Harold E. Fey.

Scottish Journal of Theology 6:97–99.

Spectator (3 October 1952): 3149. H. F.

Theologische Literaturzeitung 77:292–94. Erich Roth

Theologische Literaturzeitung 77:420–22. E. W. Zeeden.

Theology 55:313–14. T. H. L. Parker.

Theology Today 8:558–60. E. Harris Harbison.
Time (18 September 1950): 68.
Time and Tide (5 April 1952): 340.
Times Educational Supplement (8 February 1952):103.
Times Literary Supplement (3 November 1950): 697.
Tro och Liv 4:178. Nils Tägt.
Väs Lösen 52:95. Gunnar Hillerdal.
Westminster Bookman 10:24–25. Theodore G. Tappert.
Wisconsin Library Bulletin 46:20.
The Witness (11 October 1951): 7. Frederick C. Grant.
Workers with Youth 15:18.
Yale Divinity News (November 1950): 7. John W. Brush.
Yale Review 40:350. Heinz Bluhm.
*Zeitschrift für Religions- Geistesgeschichte- und
    Schriftleitung* 3:363–66. Ernst Benz.

Ernst Benz,
by RHB

P18   *The Horizon History of Christianity* (1964). See A30.
Baptist Quarterly 21:235–36. G. W. Rusting.
Best Sellers 24:275.
Biblioteca Sacra 122:277–78. G. W. Dollar.
Books Abroad 39:354. E. Copeland.
Books Today 3:13. C. Peterson.
Choice 2:100. James H. Smylie.
Christian Century 81:1536.
Columbia 44:34. D. Hughes.
International Journal of Religious Education 41:4. Virgil E. Foster.
International Journal of Religious Education 42:20. L. J. Gable.
Library Journal 89:5025.
Lutheran Libraries 7:12. Frank Munson.
New Statesman 70:20. Philip Mairet.
New York Times Book Review (6 December 1964):28. Benedict Kiely.
Perspective (Pittsburgh) 7:62.
Publishers Weekly 189:72.
Punch 248:677.
Revue d'histoire et de philosophie religieuse 46:182. B. Roussel.
Times Literary Supplement (27 May 1965): 435.
Yale Divinity News (November 1964):18.

P19   *Hunted Heretic: The Life and Death of Michael Servetus, 1511–1553* (1953).
      See A14.
      American Historical Review 59:914–16. Myron P. Gilmore.
      Annals of the American Academy of Political and Social Science 293:192.
         G. C. Boyce.
      Archiv für Reformationsgeschichte 45:127–29. Geoffrey F. Nuttall.
      Booklist 50:237.
      Bookmark 13:103.
      Bulletin of the History of Medicine 29:84.
      Christian Century 70:1326–27. W. E. Garrison.
      Church History 23:282–83. Raymond W. Albright.
      Hibbert Journal 52:210. H. L. Short.
      Isis (History of Science Society) 45:313. N. K. Bunger.
      Journal of Modern History 26:373–76. Quirinus Breen.
      New York Times (6 December 1953): sec. 7:22.
      Religion in Life 23:474–75.
      Renaissance News 7:45–46. Wilhelm Pauck.
      Theology Today 11:422–23. E. H. Harbison.
      United States Quarterly Book Review 10:148.

P20   *Luther's Meditations on the Gospels* (1962). See A27.
      Archiv für Reformationsgeschichte 54:259–60. E. Theodore Bachmann.
      Christian Century 80:1030–31. Harold J. Grimm.
      Church History 31:462–63. Edgar M. Carlson.
      Concordia Theological Monthly 34:49–50. Lewis W. Spitz.
      Lutheran Quarterly 15:283–84. Robert Esbjornson.
      Perkins School of Theology Journal 15:52–53. Victor P. Furnish.
      Religion in Life 32:638–39. Robert H. Fischer.

P21   *The Martin Luther Christmas Book* (1948). See A10.
      Christian Century 65:1369. Winfred E. Garrison.
      Church History 17:341.
      Duke Divinity School Bulletin 13:117. Ray C. Petry.
      Eden Theological Seminary Alumni Bulletin 4:4.
      Lutheran Quarterly 1:235–36. H. A. Preus.
      Mennonite Life 6:47. Cornelius Krahn.
      New York Times (18 September 1948):15.
      Review and Expositer 46:91–92.
      Westminster Bookman 8:2. Winthrop S. Hudson.
      Theologische Literaturzeitung 9:548. Hans Preus.

P21.5   *The Martin Luther Easter Book* (1983). See A37.
          Anglican Theological Review 66:293–97. Donald S. Armentraut
          Trinity Seminary Review 5:2, 15–20; 6:1 40–47; 6:2, 24–27. James L.
          Schaaf.

P22   *The Medieval Church* (1962). See A25.
          Archiv für Reformationsgeschichte 45:127–28. Geoffrey F. Nuttall.
          Church History 23:282–83.
          Religion in Life 34:150. Robert H. Fischer.
          Speculum 39:112. Marshall W. Baldwin.

P23   *The Penguin History of Christianity* (1967). See A30.
          Tablet 222:964. E. Quinn.
          Times Literary Supplement (23 January 1969): 91.

P24   *Pilgrim Parson* (1958). See A21.
          Bulletin of the Congregational Library 10:3–4.
          Christian Century 76:478. Hampton Adams.
          Yale Divinity News (November 1959):15. Robert C. Calhoun.

P24.5   *A Pilgrimage to Luther's Germany* (1983). See A38.
          Anglican Theological Review 66:293–97. Donald S.Armentraut.
          Book Newsletter of the Augsburg Publishing House 505. C. F. Weller.
          Lutheran Forum 17:32–33. G. C. Stone.

P25   *The Reformation of the Sixteenth Century* (1952). See A13.
          American Historical Review 58:345–46. G. C. Sellery.
          — RHB response: 58:1055–56.
          — Sellery's response to RHB's response: 58:1057.
          Annals of the American Academy of Political and Social Science 283–317.
          Archiv für Reformationsgeschichte 46:123–24. O. Schottenloher.
          The Beacon 2:3–4.
          Belfagor 3:344–47. Delio Cantimori.
          Booklist 48:370.
          British Weekly (22 October 1953):2. Glen Lloyd.
          Chicago Sunday Tribune (13 July 1952):2. L. T. Heron.
          Christian Century 69:724. W. E. Garrison.
          The Churchman 166:18. F. J. Moore.
          Duke Divinity School Bulletin 18:54–55. Thomas A. Schafer.
          Erasmus 6:810–12. Hubert Jedin.
          Fortnightly Review 174:67–68. B. C. Plowright.
          Hibbert Journal 51:86. W. L. Allen.

P25   *The Reformation of the Sixteenth Century* (1952) (Continued).
        History 50:222.
        Indian Journal of Theology 14:37–38. Kaj Baago.
        Kirkus 20:334.
        Life of the Spirit 8:478. R. Blundell.
        Lutheran Quarterly 5:97. Conrad Bebendoff.
        Mennonite Quarterly Review 6:323–24. Robert Friedmann.
        Methodist Recorder (7 January 1954). Gordon Rupp.
        National Council Outlook (October 1952):23. Samuel McCrea Cavert.
        The Pulpit 30:318. Charles Clayton.
        Religion in Life 21:149–51. Massey H. Shepherd, Jr.
        Spectator (18 December 1953): 746–47.
        Theology Today 9:552–53. Norman Victor Hope.
        Time and Tide (21 November 1953):1524. Frederic Hood.
        Times Literary Supplement (16 October 1953): 698.
        View-Review (November 1953):26–27. Gordon Rupp.

P25.5   *Roly* (1988). See A39.
        Church History 63:158–59. Robert H. Fischer.

P26   *The Travail of Religious Liberty* (1951). See A12.
        American Historical Review 57:488–89. Winthrop S. Hudson.
        Booklist 48:51.
        British Weekly (7 January 1954):2. Shaun Herron.
        Chicago Sunday Tribune (14 October 1951): 6. Clarence Seidenspinner.
        Christian Century 68:1344–45. W. E. Garrison.
        Christian Register 131:3. Duncan Howlett.
        Christian Science Monitor (17 October 1951): 9. R. E. Donlon.
        Church History 21:82–83. Lefferts A. Loetscher.
        The Churchman 86:210–11. J. Atkinson.
        Crozer Quarterly 29:198–99. Raymond W. Albright.
        Journal of Bible and Religion 20:213–14. C. F. Nesbit.
        Journal of Modern History 26:78–79.
        Kirkus 19:612.
        Mennonite Quarterly Review (October 1952): 324–25. Robert
            Friedmann.
        New Haven Register (7 October 1951): 8. W. H. Veale.
        New York Times (19 January 1952):13.
        Presbyterian Tribune 66:18–19.

Der Quaker: Monatsschrift der Deutschen Freunde 27:77–80.
R. E. v. Gronen.
Review and Expositor 49:75–76. T. D. Price.
Rivista di Storica e Letteratura Religiosa 1:154–59. F. Traniello.
Theology Today 9:263–64. W. Hubben.
Westminster Bookman 10:1–2. Robert T. Handy.

P27   *What Christianity Says about Sex, Love, and Marriage* (1957). See A18.
Theological Studies (Seoul) 7:190–92. (In Korean.)

P28   *Women of the Reformation from Spain to Scandinavia* (1977). See A35.
American Historical Review 83:708–709. Marinka Fousek.
Christian Century 94:1068, 1070. Robert H. Fischer.
Church History 47:334–35. Nancy Hardesty.
History: Review of New Books 6:172. K. H. Dannenfeldt.
Religious Education 73:4495. P. Washbourne.
Renaissance Quarterly 31:382–84. V. B. Halpert.
Theologische Literaturzeitung 104:671–72. H. Junghans.
Theology Today 34:320–21. Jean Lambert.

P29   *Women of the Reformation in France and England* (1973). See A33.
America 130:76. J. W. O'Malley.
Anglican Theological Review 57:250–51.
Archiv für Reformationsgeschichte 63:292–93. Elisabeth Gregorich
Gleason.
Book Newsletter of Augsburg Publishing House 446:1–2. John E. Quam.
Choice 11:654–55.
Christian Century 90:1156.
Christian Century 92:752. Carl Bangs.
Christian Century 94:1068–70. Robert H. Fischer.
Church History 44:407–408. S. H. Stephenson.
Fides et Historia 8:71–75. Fred R. Bell.
Reflection 72:14. Letty M. Russell.
Reformed Theological Review 33:55–56. R. Swanton.
Religious Education 70:343–44. Mary Ann Neevel.
Review for Religious 33:251. J. Donnelly.
Review of Politics 36:592–99. M. Weaver.
Sixteenth Century Journal 7:124. Virginia W. Beauchamp.

P30   *Women of the Reformation in Germany and Italy* (1971). See A32.
       Archiv für Reformationsgeschichte 63:292–93. Elisabeth Gregorich
          Gleason.
       Bulletin de la Société de l'Histoire de Protestantisme Française 24:356–57.
          Miriam Usher Chrisman.
       Catholic Historical Review 58:630.
       Choice 8:1298.
       Christian Century 88:1008. Marianka Fousek.
       Church History 41:261. Jill Raitt.
       Fides et Historia 8:71–75. Fred R. Bell.
       Journal of Modern History 44:251–52. Nancy L. Roelker.
       Library Journal 96:3146. L. H. Ward.
       Lutheran Libraries 14:15–16. Ellen J. Stanius.
       Lutheran Quarterly 23:407. Theodore G. Tappert.
       Religious Education 67:229–30. Mary Ann Neevel.
       Revue d'Histoire et de Philosophie Religieuse 73:345–46. Max A.
          Chevallier.
       Review of Books and Religion 1:1, 12.
       Saint Luke's Journal of Theology 15:62–63. Donald S. Armentraut.
       Sarah Lawrence College Bulletin (May 1973):267. Joan Kelly Gadol.
       Theologische Literaturzeitung 97:687–88. Ingetraut Ludolphy.
       Union Seminary Quarterly Review 28:130–34. A. Hackett.

P31   *Yale and the Ministry* (1957). See A20.
       American Historical Review 63:525. Wilson Smith.
       Chicago Theological Seminary Register 47:27–28. A. C. McGiffert, Jr.
       Christian Century 74:1319, 1322. Albert C. Outler.
       Christianity Today 2:34. John H. Gerstner.
       Church History 27:174–75. Lefferts A. Loetscher.
       Historical Magazine 27:158–59. W. Norman Pittenger.
       Harvard Divinity Bulletin 23:190–91. John Dillenberger.
       Journal of Bible and Religion 27:77. George Hunston Williams.
       Journal of Religion 38:77–78. Vincent Daniels.
       Kirkus 25:264.
       New England Quarterly (March 1958):107–109. Conrad Wright.
       New York Times (23 June 1957): sec. 7:7. Paul Ramsey.
       The Pulpit 28:29. Martin E. Marty
       Review and Expositor 54:610–11. Guy H. Ranson.
       Saturday Review of Literature 40:53. H. B.
       Theology Today 14:551–53. James Hastings Nichols

Yale Divinity News (May 1957): 9–10. Luther Weigle.

P32   *Yesterday, Today, and What's Next?* (1978). See A36.
       Christian Century 96:358. R. S. Michaelson.
       Church History 49:106–107. C. T. McIntire.
       Circle (October 1979).
       Ecumenical Review 32:209–10. E. T. Bachmann.
       Expository Times 91:31.
       Fellowship (January/February 1980). W. Richey Hogg.
       Fides et Historia (13:88–90). R. Swanstrom.
       Harvard Divinity Bulletin 9:17.
       Lutheran 17:31. George H. Straley.
       Lutheran Theological Journal 14:49–50. M. E. Schild.
       Princeton Seminary Bulletin 2:186–87.
       Saint Luke's Journal of Theology 23:300–301. A. J. Knoll.

Q. WRITINGS AND TRANSLATIONS

Q1   *Come Grow Old with Me.* 1982. Typescript. Located in Roland H. Bainton papers. (See R1) Cited by Reeves (see S2), 47 and 84.

Q2   "Unpublished Writings." Listed in Register for Roland H. Bainton Papers. Archives and Manuscripts. Special Collections. Yale Divinity School Library. (See R1) 25–27.

— 39 titles are listed and reproduced here.

SERIES III Box Folder	WRITINGS	Date	25
349	David Joris		
350-353	Erasmus of Christendom		
354	George Lincoln Burr: His Life		
355-357	Here I Stand		
25 358	The Horizon History of Christianity		
359	Hunted Heretic		
360	The Martin Luther Christmas Book		
361	The Medieval Church		
362	Pilgrim Parson		
363	The Reformation of the Sixteenth Century		
364	The Travail of Religious Liberty		
365	Ulrich von Hutten and the German Reformation (translation by RHB)		
366	Women of the Reformation		
367	Yale and the Ministry		
368	Yesterday, Today, and What Next?		
369	Reviews of RHB articles		
370	General reviews of RHB's work		
	Unpublished writings		
26 371	"Authority and Religious Knowledge" (Theol. Discussion Group)	1935	
372	"The Bible and Western Culture"	1967	
	Unpublished writings (cont'd)		
26 373,374	"Calvin and the Liberal Reformers"	n.d.	
375	"A Christ to the Neighbor"	n.d.	
375	"Christmas Behind Barbed Wire"	n.d.	
375	"Comments on Wilhelm Pauck's paper on The Idea of the Church in Christian History" (Theol. Discussion Group)	1936	
376	"Erasmus and Italy"	1967	

Page 25 of "Unpublished Writings." See Q2.

R. ARCHIVAL COLLECTIONS

R1   *Roland H. Bainton Papers.* (Archives and Manuscripts; Manuscript Group
        no. 75). Special Collections. Yale Divinity School Library, New Haven, Ct.
        Compiled by Nathan H. Price and Martha Lund Smalley. April 1992. 59
        pages. Computer-produced copy.

R2   *Quaker Miscellany, 1659–1984.* Correspondence, diaries, memoirs, essays,
        published articles, clippings, poetry, maps, geneology, wills, manumissions,
        photographs, plays, and other papers related to Quakers. 48 boxes. (Held
        by Haverford College, Haverford, Pa.)

        — RHB materials including version of "A Refugee from the Nether-
        lands: David Joris."

S. DISSERTATION, THESIS, AND PAPER ABOUT RHB

S1   Geisser, Heinrich. *Roland Bainton als Darsteller des 16. Jahrhunderts.* Semi-
        nararbeit bei Herrn. Prof. Dr. Werner Kaegi. Wintersemester 1968–69. 18
        pages. See U1.

S2   Reeves, Brian Randal. *Roland H. Bainton: The Historian as Social Activist.* A
        Thesis Submitted in Partial Fulfillment of the Requirements for the Degree
        of Master of Arts. Social Science. 1995. Northeast Missouri State Univer-
        sity [Now Truman State University], Kirksville, Missouri. 91 pages.

S3   Simpler, Steven Houston. *A Critical Analysis of the Church History Writings
        of Roland H. Bainton.* Baylor University, 1981. 287 pages.

T. PAINTING AND SCULPTURE PORTRAYING RHB

T1   Bronze bust by Valerie Peed, "a trained scuptress," who during her final
        year at Yale Divinity School did a lifesize head and shoulders model of
        RHB. The bust was presented to him on his 85th birthday in 1979. (*Roly,*
        A39, 214.)

T2   Portrait painted by Deane Keller, Professor Emeritus of Drawing and
        Painting at Yale University. Unveiled 19 February 1975. Property of Yale
        Divinity School.

        — For further information, see O24.

U. ELECTRONIC RESOURCES

As early as January 1997 a search of the World Wide Web using Netscape located 326 references to Roland H. Bainton. By early 2000, numerous Web search engines identified up to six hundred references to Bainton. His works are cited in the footnotes of papers; in bibliographies; in on-line journals such as *Comitatus: A Journal of Medieval and Renaissance Studies;* in reference sources on the Internet; and named in book lists for course listings posted by universities around the world. These references are in flux in keeping with the nature of the Internet itself. One can only imagine how Roland Bainton's own work would have been affected by this medium.

I have included here only a few locations on the World Wide Web which have particular interest. People pursuing the subject of Roland Bainton on the Internet will have to do their own immediate search to locate the latest materials available. Periodical indexes are also available in electronic form. Some have the capacity to deliver the full text of articles indexed. The future will undoubtedly see more resources from the past reproduced in electronic form making them available to a vastly larger readership than was possible when the original source was printed.

U1   *Guide to Archives and Manuscript Collections: Personal Papers.* Yale Divinity Library. World Wide Web, 20 January 1997. <http://www.library.yale.edu/div/colgpers.htm> (see R1).

    — "Bainton, Roland Herbert, (RG75). Yale professor of church history (1923–1962); correspondence, writings, course-related materials, notes, artwork, biographical documentation. (34 linear ft.)"

U2   *Media Mart Video Where Luther Walked.* Vision Video—Media Mart Selection. "Where Luther Walked." VHS-NTSC no. 105874. Vision Video no. 19.95.
<http://www.netvideo.com/mediamart/video/rel/sku/mm10587.4html>.

U3   "Roland H. Bainton," entry in *Cambridge Biographical Encyclopedia.* 1994, available on the Internet, <http://www.biography.com./biography/final/biography.index.B.html>.

U4   The University Press of Virginia Recent Awards. The winner of the Sixteenth Century Studies Conference Roland H. Bainton Book Prize for 1995 was announced via the Internet (H. C. Erik Midelfort's *Medieval Princes of Renaissance Germany*). See OM1.

INDEX

ISBN 0-943549-66-3

DATE DUE

Demco, Inc. 38-293